CHRISTIAN
WOMEN
BLESSED WHEREVER YOU GO

ROBERT MOMENT

LEGAL STATEMENT

Christian Women © 2011 by Robert Moment.

All rights reserved.

No part of this book may be used or reproduced in any manner without the express written permission of the author.

ISBN-13: 978-0-9799982-4-9

LIABILITY/WARRANTY

The views and interpretations expressed in this book are the authors, and are not intended to provide exact or specific advice. The author shall not be liable for any loss or damage incurred in the process of following advice presented in this book.

All Scripture quotations and references are from the following sources:

Holy Bible, New Living Translation (NLT), © 1996, 2004. Used by permission of Tyndale House Publishers, Inc, Wheaton, Illinois 60189. All rights reserved.

Holy Bible, Today's New International Version (TNIV) Copyright 2001, 2005 by Biblica. All rights reserved worldwide.

New International Version (NIV) Holy Bible, New International Version, Copyright 1973,1978, 1984 Biblica. Used by permission of Zondervan . All rights reserved.

The New King James Version. © 1982 by Thomas Nelson, Inc. Used by permission. All rights reserved.

21st Century King James Version, copyright © 1994. Used by permission of Deuel Enterprises, Inc. Gary, SD 57237. All rights reserved.

The Good News Bible: The Bible in Today's English Version (TEV), American Bible Society: New York, © 1976.

This book is dedicated with love and affection to my mother,
Emma Moment.
Thanks for your love and support and *always* believing in me.

I love you Mom...

Special Prayer for You
Blessed Wherever You Go

Dear Heavenly Father,

Thank You for being my friend and loving me unconditionally. Thanks for Your faithfulness. I give my whole heart to You.

Help me to love others and help me to see and love myself through Your eyes.

I choose to put You first in my life. I trust You. I trust Your plan. I trust Your goodness. I trust You with my past, present and future. I will walk by faith and not by sight.

I open my heart and mind to receive all that You have for me.

Thank You for ordering my steps and preparing me for the blessings and promotion You have in my future.

Right now, Father, I say "yes" to whatever work You have for me to do. Father, I am available for You.

Thank You for supplying all of my needs according to Your riches in glory.

Every day, I celebrate the truth that I am Your child... chosen...loved... and blessed by You.

I receive Your love for me.

In Jesus Name, Amen.

–Robert Moment

Table of Contents

Introduction 1
Let Go and Let God 5
Every Moment With God is Precious 9
God I Am Available for You 13
God Make Me Mold Me 17
The Blessings of a Mother's Love 21
God's Grace is All You Need 25
Trust in God to See You Through 29
God Wants Us to Listen to Him 33
God's Love is Unconditional and Unfailing 37
God - Where Are You 41
God Will Never Leave You 45
God is the Same Yesterday, Today and Forever 49
Waiting on God's Perfect Timing 53
God Will Never Give Up On You 59
God Gives Us Many Chances 63
Will God Speak to Me 67
God Can Lead You to Self-Discovery 71
God Can Heal Brokenness 75
Five Great Needs Only God Can Fulfill 79
The Power of God 85
Understanding the Will of God 89
God Works On Our Insides First 93
Having an Attitude of Gratitude 97
The Power of Our Testimony 101

Writing a Heartfelt Letter to God-Finding Emotional Freedom ...105
God is a Healer 109
How to Overcome Grief 113
God Uses Ordinary People to Do Extraordinary Things...............119
Rejection is God's Protection 123
How to Be Happy...127
How to Reach Your Divine Potential 131
Caregivers are God's Precious Gift to Us 135
How to Forgive Yourself 139
Who Do You Need to Forgive 147
When Your Diagnosis is Cancer-God Will Never Leave You........151
When Someone You Love Has Cancer 155
How to Pray Effectively - Seven Steps to Answered Prayers 163
God Will Diminish Our Sight to Increase Our Faith 167
Walk by Faith and Leave the Results to God 171
How to Discover Your Life's Purpose...175
The Powerful Benefits of Tithing 179
When Life Hurts - God Can Heal Your Emotional Wounds........183
Choose to Be Free from Your Past..187
Emotional Healing - Breaking Your Silence...................................191
Emotional Healing After Your Husband's Sexual Betrayal............195
Only God Needs to Know 199
Single Christian Women- 5 Things to Look for in a Partner.........203
Finding Your Path to Prosperity through God..............................207
The Proverbs 31 Woman 213
Blessed Wherever You Go 217
One Final Thought 221

Introduction

Trusting in God is the key that opens doors to be blessed wherever you go.
    –Robert Moment

Let Go and Let God. Are you ready to **Be Blessed Wherever You Go**? Your complete trust and faith in God can transform your life- spiritually, emotionally, physically and mentally. *Your life matters to God.* God has so much in store for you.

Begin each day with a "Thank You, God", in your heart and set the tone for your entire day. Choose to embrace every God-given day with a positive attitude and Celebrate God's love for you.

I pray that you feel a direct connection to God each and every day of your life and experience His love, power and blessings.

When you read '**Christian Women**,' you will learn to open your heart to the possibilities that only God can bring. It is my prayer that God will use the pages in this inspirational book to revolutionize your life.

If you are ready to experience God's blessings you can begin right now. '**Christian Women**' was written to encourage and inspire you to be God's very best. As you read the book, you will discover that you are truly a unique "Gift" to this world and there is so much value within you. It is my sincere hope to offer you support and guidance as you experience God's love and power in reading the inspirational messages.

Inside this book, '**Christian Women**,' you will learn how to:

- Personally Experience God's Blessings
- Cope with the Frustrations of Daily Living
- Forgive and Release Past Hurt and Mistakes
- Maintain Hope in the Face of Sorrow
- Endure in the Face of Overwhelming Odds
- Experience God's Healing Power
- Overcome the Pain of Guilt and Worry
- Live Your Best Life Now

By the time you finish reading '**Christian Women**,' that includes such inspirational chapters as: Trust in God to See You Through, God is the Same Yesterday, Today, and Forever, God Can Heal Brokenness, Waiting On God's Perfect Timing, Only God Needs to Know and Five Great Needs Only God Can Fulfill, you will learn that God has great things in store for you and you will believe it too. Why? Because God will use His all-encompassing power to show you things about Himself

Introduction

and you that were previously not known. You will laugh, cry, and scream at times, but there won't ever be a time that God isn't right there to take it all in with you. Don't worry – His shoulders are broad enough and His arms long and strong enough to hold you and handle whatever you have to tell Him. Trust your life to God !

My hope is that '**Christian Women**' will inspire you to find your true "self" by embracing God's love. Be Inspired and Be Blessed. May God Bless You Richly Wherever You Go!

Say out loud and declare by faith- ***I am blessed wherever I go.***

> *"I can do ALL things through Christ who strengthens me."*
>
> *–Philippians 4:13*

Let Go and Let God

As we travel on life's great journey, our minds are constantly being exposed to impediments that fill us with confusion, negativity, anger, sadness, and despair. However, the power of those negative external influences is no match for the power of God's love. To feel God's love and accept Him as your teacher, you need to empty your mind of the impediments that are preventing you from accepting the fact that God can and will perform great miracles.

God is not withholding Himself from you. He needs you to believe in Him. He will walk beside you as you journey through life once you have accepted Him.

> *"Teach me to do your will, for you are my God. Let your good spirit lead me on a level path."*
> *–Psalm 143:10*

Take a deep breath. Slowly exhale and allow your body and mind to relax. Tell yourself: I am letting go, I am letting God fill my by body and soul. Accept that God's love and wisdom is always present and available when you accept Him. God is ready to fill you with new awareness, life, light, and understanding. Let God fill the emptiness within you that brings you fear, worry, hurt, loneliness, doubt, anxiety or sadness. Let go! Let God fill you with love, happiness, joy and peace

> *"The Lord is my shepherd, I shall not want. He makes me lie down in green pastures; he leads me beside still waters."*
>
> *—Psalm 23:1-2*

Release feelings of fear, anxiety, doubt, confusion or anger in your life. Eliminate the tendency to control situations and realize God is the answer to all of your problems. You can release all matters to God with certainty. He always keeps His promises. He is faithful. God wants you to lay your burden upon Him and experience His peace. He wants you to trust Him, lean on and allow Him to carry the burden for you. Let Go and Let God and wait on His perfect timing for the circumstances or events in your life. God is never absent- He is present in any and all situations.

When you let go, God's light will come forth and await your acceptance so that you can move forward and heal. Let the positive thought shine through with God's light and let His light melt your fears, anxieties, and anger. Let Go and Let God do his work.

Start to calmly reason and question your place in this world. Feel a renewed strength and courage to step into the light and begin a new day filled with hope and promise. With a new acceptance in God, you will feel your prayers being acknowledged. You will have a better sense of God as Teacher and Guide. Feel God's light within you to find your personal strength. God supports your strength by providing faith, knowledge, healing, understanding, and any other need you have to carry you forward in life.

Whatever your life experience, God is with you at that moment and long after the experience is a distant memory. Let go of personal pains and let God move through you to fill every void so that you find the courage and faith to handle whatever obstacle life puts on your path. God's love and goodness will always help you overcome any obstacle in life. Even though it may seem challenging, God always supplies the spiritual comfort and security. Tell yourself: God will NOT desert or forsake me, His own creation.

God's love and wisdom is ever nurturing your soul by making the dark places light, rough patches smooth, and vacant places full again. Let Go and Let God and relax and enjoy the view as God leads the way to the blessings that are yours.

Every Moment With God is Precious

Most of us know that time with God can be uplifting and we sometimes vow to spend more time in the future praying or attending church so that we can draw closer to Him, but so often, life simply gets in the way. We find ourselves thinking that the time we spend in church or at Bible study or even meditating in our own homes is time that could be spent doing other, more "practical" things that need to be taken care of. What we need to remember is that every moment with God is special.

Skipping prayer, church, meditation or Bible time for earthly things is turning your back on the one thing you need most in your life – the Lord's guidance and blessings. In fact, the more practical things you have to take care of, the more you need to have God in your every day life! God will help you to gain the earthly things you need through His guidance and blessings. His power is a transformative power that means no moment spent with Him is wasted.

Besides, God is a constant presence even after prayer and praise has ceased. He is an unwavering source of healing, harmonizing energy in our lives if we pray to Him and ask Him to enter our lives. He will answer those prayers and become a precious presence that makes every aspect of our lives special – but we must open our eyes and our hearts to see it and feel it.

> *"Seek the Lord and his strength, seek his presence continually."*
>
> *–1 Chronicles 16:11*

We sometimes make the mistake of thinking that the experience of our Creator is only in the structured moments – formal worship ceremonies, prayer, reading the Bible – but any moment that acknowledges His hand in creation and the wonder of His love for mankind can be a moment of communion with His loving kindness. These personal, private moments are just as precious in His sight as the grand gestures and hold great meaning. There is an old Irish proverb that explains the importance of small moments in a day, and they sum up how God might look at these moments as well:

> *Take the time to be friendly, it is the road to happiness;*
> *Take time to look around, the day is too short to be selfish;*
> *Take time to laugh, it is the music of the soul.*
>
> *–Irish Proverb*

We could easily add, "Take time to admire nature, it is God's handiwork," and "Take time to thank God for this day, it is His precious gift to you," and so many other phrases that would take just a few seconds out of the day. Yet each would be a precious moment with God that would enrich your personal relationship with Him.

God is our strength, our comforter and our guide. God's presence is a constant and uninterrupted power. We don't have to wait for a clear, sunny day to experience our Creator. He surrounds and enfolds us in His loving arms in countless ways that we only have to open our hearts and minds to, acknowledging just how precious each of those moments are to Him and to ourselves.

God I Am Available for You

The title above is a phrase that warms God's heart every time He hears it. In fact, the greatest gift we can give to the Lord is our service to Him, but many of us just go through the motions. When we say, "God, I'm available to you," do we really mean it, or are we secretly hope that we won't get called on in some way that will interfere with the lives we chosen for ourselves?

> *"Commit to the Lord whatever you do, and your plans will succeed."*
>
> *–Proverbs 16:3*

The key to truly being available to God is having a heart of surrender and sacrifice. Be bold! Don't stop there! After you tell the Lord you are available, ask Him what He wants you to do! Open up your heart to the many possibilities to serve Him that are available in this world.

Submitting to God's will is the ultimate sacrifice to the Lord, and one that can foster change in others. Remember that when we don't make ourselves available to God, it is harder for Him to touch our spirits.

What if God were as unavailable to us as we sometimes are to Him? It can be difficult to take on the mantle of sacrifice and allow God's plan for us to take shape. Sometimes God takes us into uncomfortable places where our beliefs may be questioned or where others may spurn our attempts to reach out to them. But think about God's experience with humankind. How often have we turned our back on God, ignored His wisdom, and even shut out His love?

We must stop ignoring God's plan for us and make ourselves fully available to Him, just as He is always fully available to us. We must also mean every word we say when we promise Him, "God, I am available to you." We can't simply be spectators to God's work on earth – we have to be fully involved.

> *"I heard the voice of the Lord saying, 'Whom shall I send? And who will go for us?' And I said, 'Here am I. Send me!'"*
>
> *–Isaiah 6:8*

There is an old saying that, "Life is not a spectator sport." Neither is being a Christian! We must live the lives God has planned for us, and the only way to do that is to jump in with both feet and *live* God's word, not simply study it. When we become active participants in God's plan, we are making ourselves available as a tool to further His kingdom.

Is it always comfortable to hear God's voice and heed His call? Of course not, but this is what makes the journey of becoming an active Christian so exhilarating. As we move forward, making ourselves available to God, we will grow in our faith and soon we will discover that we have become better, stronger Christians – all because we said, "Yes!" to God, then kept on going!

So today, pray not only for God's guidance, but to let Him know that you are here for Him, just as He is here for you. Honestly lay down your own agenda and become open to what God desires of you. When He leads you in a particular direction for His sake, don't forsake Him. Don't let your own needs or desires override your commitment to be available to the Lord. When we take that step to say, "Here I am! Send me!" we'll soon discover that the rewards for being completely available to God are infinite and far greater than what we could have imagined for ourselves.

God Make Me Mold Me

God always sees us as His precious gifts, priceless treasures in His Kingdom. Why does He see us this way? Because we are created in His image – and nothing could be more precious and special than to be created in the image of God Himself, the Lord of all creation!

This is why we must always keep in mind that He is always shaping us and conforming us to His character. He wants us to become more like Him in every way. God is the potter and we are the clay that He shapes to His own purposes, making us into worthy vessels to be filled with His Holy Spirit. When we submit and surrender our will to our Heavenly Father, He will shape and mold us according to His will and more closely to His image every day.

This growth and change as God molds us is a process that is on-going, so we do not need to be discouraged along the way. We can enjoy each step along the way. It's okay to take pleasure in where we are on our walk with God while knowing that God is not finished with us yet. He is always in the process of changing us and taking us to where He wants us to be. Simply remember that He is always working on us, from the inside out, and take solace in the fact that we can love our God with all our hearts because He continues to make us better people even as He loves us where we are right now.

> *"The Lord said to him, "Who gave man his mouth? Who makes him deaf or mute? Who gives him sight or makes him blind? Is it not I, the Lord? Now go; I will help you speak and will teach you what to say."*
>
> —*Exodus 4:11-12*

How Does God Mold Me?

But how does God mold you into the person He wants you to be? How are we to recognize the Lord's touch as He takes the unfinished clay of our lives and turns it into a beautiful, finished container for His Spirit? The simple answer is that God molds us every day, in every way.

Every contact you have with others impacts your life in some way, whether to teach you a lesson about God's mercy and love, or to strengthen your humility and resolve. There is no relationship you have that isn't part of God's molding and shaping process in some way. Each person that touches your life leaves a mark on the pottery of your soul. If you would like to move closer to God and help Him in His desire to make you a worthy vessel, associate with other Christians, for they will also help God mold you and shape you through their example and Christian love.

God also shapes you through what you do. The more you act and live like a Christian, the more God will guide your footsteps in the right path. It is a natural progression that the more you do that is kind and right and good, the more you will desire to do these things. So look to God for His support and He will give it, and shape your heart to guide you in the path of His goals and hopes for you. Because He created you, He knows everything about you and will guide you in His ways.

> *"I praise you because I am fearfully and wonderfully*
>   *made; your works are wonderful,*
> *I know that full well.*
> *My frame was not hidden from you*
> *When I was made in the secret place.*
> *When I was woven together in the depths of the*
>   *earth,*
> *Your eyes saw my unformed body.*
> *All the days ordained for me*
> *Were written in your book*
> *Before one of them came to be."*
>
> *–Psalm 139:14-16*

The Blessings of a Mother's Love

God bless you, Dear Mothers of the world! Whether you have given birth or have assumed the role of mother in some other way, know that you are loved and honored for everything you have done and continue to do in our lives by nurturing, loving and caring for your children and all of God's children.

Sometimes it may be difficult to believe that you are so exalted. Your children may take you for granted, society values your achievements in the workforce more than what you do at home, and even your husband may neglect to thank you. But God never forgets! He knows that you love unconditionally, encourage against all odds, believe in your children when no one else does. The Lord sees that you support us, listen to us, pray for us.

You shape us, correct us, and lead us in the right paths. In fact, you are the closest thing there is to Jesus' pure love on earth! No one else sacrifices as much, or as willingly, as a Mother does for her child. She will go to the ends of the earth, fight the powers of this world, and willingly die for her child. She is a living example of Jesus' sacrificial love every day.

Think of Mary, the Mother of God. She knew her son would sacrifice Himself for the world, yet she did not try to stop Him. Instead, she sat at the foot of the cross when He was crucified, mourning His suffering, yet never leaving Him. Mothers will stand by their children to the end, even when they know they cannot change the ending. Why? Because the love of a Mother, like the love of God, is infinite in its depth and passion. In fact, Jesus loved His earthly mother so much that He told His disciples to look out for her after He was gone:

"Near the cross of Jesus stood His mother, his mother's sister, Mary the wife of Clopas, and Mary Magdalene. When Jesus saw His mother there, and the disciple whom He loved standing nearby, he said to His mother, "Dear woman, here is your son," and to the disciple, "She is your mother."
—John 19:25-27

In most families, Mothers are the "keeper of the gates," they give us our religious instruction and guide us on the path to God. Mothers teach us to say our bedtime prayers when we are little children. They take us to church each Sunday and show us by their example how to lead Christian lives. Perhaps Mothers do this because they are uniquely qualified to understand the nature of God's sacrificial love. They live that kind of love each and every day – sacrificing their own lives for their children in countless ways.

God is all-powerful and perfect in His wisdom – and He determined that life should be created out of women. Without Mothers, life could not go on. He knew before the beginning of time that no one was better suited to the role than women, with their tender hearts and strong souls. Think of the powerful force your mother has been in your own life, and thank the Lord for mothers!

For those who are Mothers, we give our thanks knowing there is no expiration date on your jobs. Words can't express how much we love and honor you. May God continue to bless you as you have blessed us!

> *"Charm is deceitful and beauty is passing, but a woman who reveres the Lord will be praised."*
> *—Proverbs 31:30*

God's Grace is All You Need

People talk a lot of about the Grace of God and being touched by God's Grace, but it's one of the most difficult concepts for most of us to understand. After all, how can we grasp the concept of being the recipients of such an amazing and wonderful gift as the Grace that is God's forgiveness of our sins when we are so undeserving? And what does that Grace do to change the reality of our daily lives anyway? The answers are amazing and truly reflect just how much God loves us and the great good He desires for us.

> *"My grace is sufficient for you, for my power is made perfect in weakness..."*
>
> *—2 Corinthians 12:9*

God's Grace was given to us even before we were born, at the very beginning of time, so we know that it isn't based on whether we've earned it or if we've done something to earn it:

> *"This grace was given to us in Christ Jesus before the ages began."*
>
> *—2 Timothy 1:9*

It's so wonderful that God has always loved us and always will, and freely gave us this gracious, bountiful gift. It's an unearned blessing, a gift from our Lord and Savior that we received before we even looked for it. God's will for you is absolute good. I know this is true for myself, and I also know it is true for every person on Earth. God's love is unconditional a Grace available to everyone, at all times and in all circumstances. No matter who we are or what we've done!

That's right - you've already "earned" God's Grace simply by being a precious, individual creation of God. Simply by existing as His creation, you are deserving of His Grace ! Nothing you do or do not do can remove that Grace from your life. It is present here, now and always. Through God's Grace, you are accepted and loved in every moment. Through God's Grace you are continually blessed - and our knowledge of this constant blessing is what can change the reality of our daily lives. What could possibly bring us more joy and peace than knowing that nothing can separate us from God's Grace? No matter how low we fall or how high we climb, His Grace will surround us.

> *"Let us therefore approach the throne of Grace with boldness, so that we may receive mercy and find grace to help in time of need."*
>
> *– Hebrews 4:16*

God's Grace is All You Need

When we need God's Grace and loving kindness, we can rest assured that it will be there for us. We will be enfolded in it and can rely on it to carry us through no matter how difficult our trials, because that Grace is sufficient for every need. When we have God's Grace, we don't need the forgiveness of others or the understanding of men.

We have all that we need to carry us through the problems in our lives, and the realization that our God has showered us with His Grace all our lives and He will never withhold it should embolden us - it is our guarantee that we can do anything ! With the Grace of God shielding us, what amazing things we can do with our own lives and in the lives of others, what riches we can share ! That Grace gives meaning and glory to our lives as members of the body of Christ's church on earth - we should share that Grace with others. It is all that we will ever need to find peace in our lives, and by sharing it with those around us, that joy and peace will be magnified to the Glory of God.

> *"Grace to you and peace from God our Father and the Lord Jesus Christ."*
>
> *–1 Corinthians 1:3*

With an attitude of gratitude, we live our daily lives in the very atmosphere of God's Grace. God's will for us is absolute good.

God's love is unending, a grace that is for all, at all times and in all circumstances.

Trust in God to See You Through

"You will never truly know faith, yourself and God until you have been tested by adversity"
—Robert Moment

God can make a way out of no way. There are times in life when we hit a dead end and feel as though we are out of options. We've been brought low by fate or circumstance or even by our own wrong choices and we feel like we just can't go on. These are the times when we just aren't sure that God can really be there for us because things look so grim. It seems like that cloud over our head is raining down nothing but more pain and suffering on us and we just don't see how God can lead us through all of the suffering we see. This is when we have to put our faith in God and understand that God is unique in the universe - He can see us through anything, no matter how bad the problem, no matter how low we are, no matter how bad we feel !

We all go through challenging times in our lives emotionally, financially, psychologically and spiritually. But we can trust in God to see us through. God is as close as the call of His Name. No matter how low we've fallen or how depressed we are, God has the power to save our lives. Be willing to put your trust and faith in God and put aside your pride; be willing to humble yourself and cry out to God for help from the depths of your heart and soul.

You may be asking yourself, "How do I know God can see me through *my* problem?" Remember, God has been here since the beginning of time and the world itself. From where we sit, our problems may seem insurmountable, but from where He sits as Ruler of the Universe, our problems aren't insurmountable at all. In fact, like a loving Father, He sees each of our problems and understands them. In His compassion and wisdom, He is simply waiting for each of us to come to Him and say, "Father, please help me to get through this. I need You."

Then remember that if you want God to see you through, you must trust Him ! And trust can be difficult when times are dark and life is difficult. Sometimes we want an easy fix and quick results. If our prayers aren't answered immediately, we wonder if God is really listening. Be faithful and understand that God, in His wisdom, knows what is best for you and that He knows what you have the strength to endure in the days ahead - and that He will always be with you. ***Trust*** in Him and He will ***see you through !***

Turn to God in prayer and meditation and release your concerns about this day and the days ahead - turn them over to Him and He will help you to see them through. Just say,

"God, I trust you to be my guide and inspiration and to see me through whatever challenging circumstances I may have to face in the days ahead." In the Psalms, the Lord reminds us of just how much He loves us and how much He wants to be a part of our daily lives, seeing us through our daily struggles and being a part of our daily triumphs,

> *"The Lord says, "I will guide you along the best pathway for your life. I will advise you and watch over you"*
>
> *–Psalm 32:8*

Did God promise that the way would always be easy? No. But he DID promise that He would always be there to guide you along the best pathway to guide you and watch over you.

God Wants Us to Listen to Him

God is bigger than any problem we will ever face and He can guide us through all of our trials and sorrows, but first we must listen to Him. We can talk to God any time and about anything – in fact, that's sometimes the easy part. The challenge is in knowing how to *listen* to God. Whether you are a teenager facing peer pressure or an adult facing chemical dependency, a life threatening disease, unemployment or loneliness, we can talk to God and reveal the burdens of our heart. And God will listen to those sorrows and give us comfort!

But beyond simply confessing our sorrows and praying for comfort, the Lord wants us to ask Him questions. When we ask for guidance or God's direction, we are letting Him know that we seek the answers He is so anxious to give us. What should I do? How do I carry on? What is Your will for my life? These are all questions that God will answer if you are willing to truly open a listening heart! God has all of the answers we need if we will only listen to Him.

Sometimes the answers we seek reveal themselves immediately, while at other times they come at a time and in a manner that's unexpected and disconcerting. We may struggle against what the answer is, but God's love for us is patient – He will keep offering His answers and wait for us to listen. He won't abandon us if we refuse to hear the first time or even the tenth time! You see, God loves us so much that He is willing to give us the answers over and over until we are ready to receive them.

But how do we learn to truly listen and accept God's answers for our lives? First, we must realize that listening so that we truly *hear* God's call is the most important thing in our lives. If we are too busy with the hustle and hurry of our everyday lives, we may not hear because God's voice is drowned out by the world's confusion. You must set aside time to *listen* and *hear*.

"Be Still and Know that I am God."
—Psalm 46:10

We need to tune out the noise and distraction of this world and allow God's voice to reach us within our hearts and souls. It isn't always easy to do this – we have to take the time to focus on God within this busy, noisy world. But no matter what time of day or night we turn to Him with a listening heart, He will be waiting for you.

These simple steps will help you open up to what God wants to say:

1. **Train yourself to hear the Lord by reading your Bible, which is the Word of God.** His Word will open your heart and your ears to the sound of His voice and His desire for you.

2. **Look for and listen to God's words in the world around you.** As you open your heart, you will be amazed by the many signs of God's love for you that surround you even in the gravest of circumstances.

3. **Give yourself over to God's will.** You may hear the word of God and be afraid of what He has planned for you and you may want to turn away – but ignoring God's plan when you have heard it is worse than never having heard it at all. The most important part of hearing is truly *listening to* God! And listening requires a heart and soul that are ready to receive God wholeheartedly.

Are you ready to listen to God? Then talk to Him and open your heart so that it is ready when God speaks to you!

> *"Listen to advice and accept instruction, that you may gain wisdom for the future".*
> *—Proverbs 19:20*

God's Love is Unconditional and Unfailing

God loves you with a steadfast and enduring love that can be difficult to understand but is pure joy to rely on. "O my strength to you I sing praises, for you, O God, are my refuge, the God who shows me unfailing love" (Psalm 59:17).

But what does God mean by unfailing love? As humans, we understand through our faith that God is our comfort and our strength, but do we really know in our deepest heart that he loves us unconditionally, without fail and without change? It can be difficult to fathom this whole-hearted, unreserved love. After all, even those closest to us may sometimes let us down or grow away from us.

Perhaps the only love on earth that is close to God's unconditional love is the love a parent have for their children. We will protect them to the very end of our days, comfort them when they are hurting and defend them even when they have disappointed or exasperated us. God's love for us is the same - we do not have to perform or live up to certain expectations to receive His love. In our personal lives, we may always strive to be good enough, interesting enough or attractive enough - but with God, the love is there from the beginning and is steadfast and unfailing even when we are at our worst.

God's Love is Always Present

God says, "When you call Me, I will answer." That's a pretty strong affirmation. He doesn't say, "Call Me and I'll get back to you," or "call Me and if I'm not angry with you I'll answer." There are no limitations, no strings attached, just a simple and pure promise. This is what unconditional love is about - it is all about God being there for you, day and night, year after year, during the highs and the lows of your life. Will you always get the answer you want? Probably not, but then God, like a good parent, knows what is best for you. His answers are the right ones and He will always provide them out of love for you.

God knows you better than anyone else. Does that sound frightening to you? It shouldn't. Yes, God knows about all of the small sacrifices you've made as well as the big mistakes - and His love changes *not one bit* because of them ! If you can accept God's love and the good He has prepared for you in the same manner it was given - unconditionally and without reservation - you will find peace in knowing that unconditional love.

The Comfort of Unconditional Love

If you've ever had a friend or loved one that you felt you could trust completely, you've had a faint taste of what it like to be

God's Love is Unconditional and Unfailing

able to rely on someone without worry or fear. But even the strongest relationships can end, loved ones can die, circumstances can destroy our faith in others. Not so with God and His unconditional love because He is never-ending and never changing. Nothing in this world that you can do or say will alter His love for you. He will never leave you or forsake you. You can always, always find comfort and security through your relationship with God because it is, like Him, eternal. "Even though I walk through the dark valley of death, I will not be afraid for you are close beside me. Your rod and your staff protect and comfort me" (Psalm 23:4). Isn't it a wonderful feeling to know that, just like the writer of the Psalm, God's presence and love are still here today, still an eternal presence in your life?

No matter what you do, no matter how you look, no matter how many mistakes you've made; you can never let God down because He love you without conditions, without measure and with no reservations. God is guiding you through every experience of your life - not because you have earned it, but because God loves you no matter what. When the dark clouds settle and all others abandon you, the light of God will shine bright and show you the way. His guiding light is unconditional love.

God - Where Are You

Trusting in the Lord can be difficult during the lowest times in our lives. Sometimes we face trials that are frightening or go through painful or sorrowful situations that make us wonder why God seems to be hiding His face from us. What we need to remember is that God isn't hiding from us – He isn't the reason that we have fallen on hard times or that our lives have been hit by sorrow or loss. In fact, He is the one constant we can rely on to get us through our trials and tribulations !

When things happen in our lives that are upsetting or unfortunate, we sometimes say, God, where are you?" Things seem to be getting worse instead of better and we wonder why God allows bad things to happen to us. We have to keep in mind that God isn't punishing us or sending us trials or punishments – the world is filled with problems and troubles. God is still present in our lives to lift us up and give us hope despite the troubles of our daily lives. We simply have to let go and let God into the events of our lives so that everything can come together in the perfect order that He has planned for us.

> *"The Lord is good, a refuge in times of trouble. He cares for those who trust in him."*
>
> *–Nahum 1:7*

The next time you are suffering, whether it is because of some personal grief, a lost job, financial worries, illness or some other issue, don't ask God where He is. Keep in mind that God is *always* there for you. He is not the reason behind your suffering, but the One who will give you refuge and strength to see you through. Pray that His love and guidance will sustain you and ask for His strength to uphold you. Say this prayer:

"Dear Heavenly Father:

I trust You. I trust Your plan. I trust Your goodness. I trust what You can see and I can't. Heavenly Father, I trust You with all things in my life and know that You will see me through this difficult time in my life with Your loving kindness. Thank You for being there in all things. **In Jesus' Name, Amen"**.

When you commune with the Lord, don't ask God where He is, because He is always there, right beside you. Instead, ask the Lord questions that can help you learn and grow as one of His children. Ask God, "What should I do, Lord, as I face these difficulties? What do you want me to learn from my sorrows? Will you help me to be strong in your love?" If you remember to walk in faith and ask God the right questions, He will answer in that still, soft voice in the night that comforts you just when you thought He wasn't there.

The world may attack us, but with God we will not be defeated. Our life may be filled with sorrow or difficulties, but with God we will never be abandoned. We may be brought low, but we will never be defeated – because God is always there.

> *"The Lord is near to all who call on Him, to all who call on Him in truth.*
> *He fulfills the desires of those who fear him;*
> *He hears their cry and saves them.*
> *The Lord watches over all who love Him."*
> *—Psalm 145:18-20*

In, God we have unparalleled hope and courage. God is the One Presence, the One Power in the universe. The spirit of God is with us, and all is well.

God Will Never Leave You

You have probably heard people say that God is always with you. That's a hard concept to understand, isn't it? But it should be a comforting one - you are secure in God's abiding presence because He is eternal, and is eternally present in your life. Because God is eternal, He has been there since the beginning of your life and will be there to see it through to the end - a promise of His love, guidance and protection that no one else can make ! Isn't it a joy to know that you can rely on Him to be there, a guiding force and comfort no matter what, for as long as you live and into the eternal?

Sometimes He may *seem* far away, perhaps because you are going through a difficult time or because you've been too busy to go to church for a few Sundays or because you've felt too unhappy to pray properly. That's okay, because even when you feel like God's face is hidden from you, He is still watching over you. *You* aren't hidden from *Him* ! Even when the sun is hidden by the clouds, it is still there, keeping the earth in its orbit.

God is never far away, even when you don't feel close to Him because you are upset or feel sorrow - because God isn't in a far away Heaven in the clouds. God's Spirit is within you and accompanies you everywhere you go. St. Patrick wrote a hymn that went,

> *"Christ be with me, Christ within me,*
> *Christ behind me, Christ before me,*
> *Christ beside me, Christ to win me,*
> *Christ to comfort me and restore me,*
> *Christ beneath me, Christ above me."*

St. Patrick understood that God's Spirit permeates our souls and wasn't a distant, impersonal presence far away from us. There is strength that comes from knowing that God's spirit is within you and accompanies you everywhere you go.

Remind yourself that God will never leave you and you will have the courage to face anything. God's presence isn't conditional - it isn't based on how good we are or whether we've gone to church or whether we've done something really wrong this month. God is simply always there, always loving us, always waiting for us to reach out to Him, ready to catch us when we fall.

Every morning before you start your day, say the following prayer for protection by James Dillet Freeman:

> *"The light of God surrounds me;*
> *The love of God enfolds me;*
> *The power of God protects me;*
> *The presence of God watches over me.*
> *Wherever I am, God is!"*

God is your ever-present help through it all. Where you are, God is and all is well.

> *"Don't be afraid, for I am with you. Do not be dismayed, for I am your God. I will help you. I will uphold you with my victorious right hand".*
> —Isaiah 41:10

God *never* abandons you because He is within you. He doesn't promise to be with you if you do this or that, He doesn't tell you *when* He will be with you. He simply says, "I am with you." And that is everything you will ever need!

God is the Same Yesterday, Today and Forever

The most powerful weapon against fear and worry is scripture. You can find a scripture that pertains to your circumstances no matter what they are and lean on their power to reassure you. But why are the words of the Bible so much more powerful than others? It's because the Word of God has been unchangeable down through the centuries, unchangeable and reliable at all times.

The God who delivered the Israelites yesterday will deliver you today and your children tomorrow. God's love, power and almighty presence are unceasing. What a wonderful and reassuring feeling!

> *"For I am the Lord, I do not change."*
> *—Malachi 3:6*

Change happens all around us; day changes to night, the seasons change, and the circumstances of our lives change. One day we may be up and the next day, down. Even those who love us most change as the days, weeks and years pass. God was wise enough to understand that we are human and that change in our lives should be part of the human condition, yet He also gave us certain constants in our lives – yes, there are seasons, but they follow a predictable pattern so that crops can grow and we can appreciate the beauty of nature. Day always follows night so that we can rest when we need to and wake up each day feeling refreshed. There is a *constancy* to even the changes in our lives that tell us that God's love is always present.

Knowing that our universe is put together so that we can rely on it to follow a reliable pattern is reassuring. It tells us that God himself is constant in His love for us, so we need not fear. His loving kindness is eternal and never changing. Even as our lives change, jobs come and go, and relationships grow and fade, God is steadfastly loving us and watching over us.

> *"Give all your worries to god, for he cares what happens to you."*
>
> *–1 Peter 5:7*

When something in our lives goes wrong or brings us sorrow, we sometimes tell ourselves, "Don't worry, this too shall pass." It is a thought that helps us to feel just a little bit better about the lows in our lives, but when the highs come along, we don't want to think that they are only temporary. It is reassuring to remember that God has promised to always be there – He is not temporary and His love will never pass away from our lives.

God is the Same Yesterday, Today and Forever

God's love, power and protection are never-changing and never-ending, no matter what we do or what happens in the universe. We don't have to tell ourselves that things will change when we think about God – He's always been there and always will be. God's mighty presence is with us in all circumstances and conditions, in all places at all times. Any adversity that we face gives God another opportunity for us to experience His great peace, love and understanding. How wonderful that the Lord is so constant – you never have to worry about whether He is there for you or not – He is eternal, just as He has always said.

> *"Do not be afraid or discouraged, for the Lord is the one who goes before you. He will be with you; he will neither fail you nor forsake you."*
> —*Deuteronomy 31:8*

Waiting on God's Perfect Timing

Waiting is one of the most difficult things to do, whether we're waiting for an airline flight, a phone call or an answered prayer. We become impatient and wonder why everyone else is holding us up and keeping us from getting what we want. It seems like the more we want something, the harder it is to wait – and we even get impatient with God!

But we have to remember that God's timing is different than our own. He sees things from a different perspective and sees the whole picture, not just what we want, but what is best for us in the grand plan for our lives. All is part of a divine order and will be done in its own right and proper time. Of course, when we are hoping, praying and waiting for something, it's easy to forget this. After all, waiting is "remaining inactive in one place while expecting something." And being inactive means feeling powerless and at the mercy of the world – nobody likes that feeling. But we must keep in mind God's greater plan and His perfect timing:

> *"We know that all things work together for good for those who love God, who are called according to His purpose."*

–Romans 8:28

"Trust in Him at all times, O people."

–Psalm 62:8

What are YOU Waiting For?

What are you waiting for in your life? A new job, financial security, healing, a baby, a restored marriage? It seems that no matter where we are in our lives, we are waiting for something in the future. Our lives are never stagnant; if we are moving forward, there is always something to expect or wait for around the next bend in the road of our lives.

There are many stories of "waiting" in the Bible. In some stories, the waiting seemed to last forever, while others only waited a few intense moments. The key to waiting is not the length of time but how we handle the wait. The Bible teaches us that we should "wait on the Lord." We must look with confidence and expectation toward the future, trusting that God will fulfill our waiting in good and proper time.

There are three actions that will help you wait on the Lord patiently and with faith, knowing and believing that He will help:

1. **Trust** – If we doubt God's willingness to hear and answer our prayer, we may begin to feel bitter when we think God has heard our prayer but is silent. Scripture teaches us that God is unchangeable, which means He is the same yester-

day, today and tomorrow and we can *always* rely on Him to provide the best possible path for our lives! God said that He will never leave us or forsake us. If He seems silent now, it is because He has another plan, different timing or a way to answer our prayer that has not been revealed to us yet. We must *trust* in His plan.

2. **Resist** – We must resist the temptation to take matters into our own hands. Patience is powerful. Having patience is essential in many circumstances and the Holy Spirit is here to fill us with this patience when we feel we cannot wait another minute on God. The safest place we can rest is in God's Will. When we rest here, resisting temptation is easy.

3. **Pray** – How many times have you given a prayer request to God and felt He was deaf? During these times, you need to *keep on praying,* but pray *the right way.* God always answers our prayers, but it may not be the way we want Him or expect Him to. It may be a yes, a no or something better. When we don't immediately get the answer we want, we have a tendency to repeat the same prayer over and over until we either lose our voice or simply give up. After we have given our need to the Lord, we must turn our request into a "Thank you," and an attitude of expectancy, and say, "Not my will, but Yours, Lord." When we thank the Lord in advance for answering our prayers, it is an active

display of our faith that demonstrates to God our confident expectation that His awesome power will provide for us.

This Prayer can help you as you wait on God's perfect timing:

Dear Heavenly Father,

Thanks for your love and always being with me.

I have been waiting for (fill-in-the-blank) for so long.

I put my complete trust in You for whatever the answer may be and whenever that answer may come in my life.

Father increase my faith and patience as I wait on Your perfect timing.

Thank you that You hear my prayers and will answer in Your time and in Your way.

Thank you for Your unfailing word and that You always keep Your promises to me.

I believe with my heart, mind and soul Your plan for my life is the best one possible and I thank You for Your answer.

Being in Your will is the safest place I can ever reside.

I receive your answered prayer Lord, because You are without limits.

In Jesus' Name, Amen.

Waiting on God's Perfect Timing

We affirm God's Perfect Timing . Trusting in God, to see His will and perfect order unfold in our lives.

God Will Never Give Up On You

God has provided each of us with spiritual gifts and graced us all with the ability to love and forgive ourselves and others. The problems we have stem from our own inability to use these gifts and our unwillingness to give in to the love and forgiveness in order to make our lives whole. It's a part of our human nature to be suspicious and give up on ourselves because we are afraid that others have given up on us. Or if they haven't given up on us yet, they just might give up on us in the future.

After all, we think, we don't have the patience to endlessly forgive and love everyone, so how can we depend on others to do the same for us? We all remember someone in our lives who let us down so often that we gave up on them in disgust. Perhaps it was someone who lied to us so often that we no longer believed them when they made a promise. Or a loved one who swore he or she would change, but we no longer thought it was possible because they'd failed so many times before. When we've been lied to, cheated on or let down by others, it destroys our ability to believe in others. By the same token, it destroys our ability to believe that anyone could ever possibly believe completely and without reservation in us.

But God is different. We don't have to prove ourselves to him. No matter how many times we fail or fall short of the goal, He will forgive us and love us. He is our comfort and strength. We need never go it alone, for the presence and love of God is our constant companion and doesn't depend upon our own actions or whether we've "proven" ourselves trustworthy or "good enough." In God's eyes, we will always be Loved.

> *"The Lord protects the simple; when I was brought low, he saved me."*
>
> *–Psalm 116:6*

That eternal love of God, based not on what we do or don't do, is one of the most precious gifts in the universe. Just imagine – God's love is unconditional. That means that no matter how many lies you tell, no matter how many times you let Him down or break a promise to Him, God will never give up on you! This should give you amazing strength and confidence. You are loved! You will always be loved – and nothing will ever change that love!

Remember Christ's last words to His disciples, all hard working, simple men who made many mistakes while trying to follow in his footsteps. When He appeared to His disciples after the crucifixion, He reminded them that they had much work to do in God's name, but they were frightened and confused. But He wasn't disappointed in them and He didn't desert them. Before going to His father in heaven, He reminded them of the most important thing that we must all keep in mind to keep us strong in our faith,

> *"Remember, I am with you always, to the end of the age."*
>
> *—Matthew 28:20*

With God always with you, even to the end of time, it becomes easier to believe in ourselves and in others. After all, if the Lord will never give up on us, who are we to give up on ourselves? Know, then, that with God, you can be successful in all that matters.

God Gives Us Many Chances

It can be difficult to stay on the right path even after we've accepted Christ into our lives. There are so many temptations around us and it's easy to stumble and fall, but we don't need to worry when we make mistakes. God gives us as many chances as we need to get our lives right and doesn't hold our mistakes against us.

God is not a God of first, second or third chances. He is a God of unlimited chances! How many chances has He given you? I have lost count of how many chances God has given me. He continues to love me, protect me and give me comfort in times of sorrow despite the numerous times I've made poor decisions and turned my back on His plans for me. Each time I've come back to Him, He has welcomed me with an open heart full of love.

The God of the Bible is a God of many chances. Moses made many mistakes; so did the prodigal son; even Paul began life as Saul, a man who repeatedly turned his back on God. But God had a plan for each of these people and gave them as many chances as they needed to make the right choice and step into God's loving embrace. He will welcome you with joy and celebrate your return to Him, no matter how many mistakes you have made.

> *"My son, the father said, you are always with me, and everything I have is yours. But we had to celebrate and be glad, because this brother of yours was dead and is alive again; he was lost and is found."*
>
> *–Luke 15: 31*

We're fortunate that God doesn't look at our lives like a baseball game – three strikes and you're out. If He did, all of us would have long ago struck out. Thankfully, God isn't a pitcher throwing us curveballs in life. Instead, life throws us lots of unexpected balls, but God never stops giving us another chance at bat. We could be abusing alcohol or drugs, facing financial failure, on parole, divorced, going through foreclosure, or simply making bad decisions in our daily lives and God will still be waiting for us. No matter how many mistakes we make, God gives us opportunities to do right by Him and ourselves every time.

In fact, God is so amazing that He turns our mistakes into opportunities to teach us! He looks on us in sorrow and love and gently corrects us when we make mistakes. He directs us, corrects us and gives us valuable lessons through our suffering when we make mistakes. In this way, He perfects us. When we make a mistake, God leads us back to the path He has laid out for us whenever we let Him.

Don't be afraid to ask God for His forgiveness and guidance when you realize you've made a mistake – He loves you and will lead you along the right path – the one He has chosen for you. Start believing that God loves you enough to forgive you and give you as many chances as you need. Ask Him to give you the chance that you need right now and begin living a life of God's purpose for you. Until you do this, you have not used your chances in life properly to fulfill His wishes for you.

> *"For I know the plans I have for you, says the Lord. They are plans for good not disaster to give you a future and a hope."*
>
> *–Jeremiah 29:11*

When you accept His offer of another chance at a Godly life, you are giving Him the glory He deserves and being given hope in return. What a wonderful exchange!

Will God Speak to Me

As we seek God's guidance, we sometimes think it would be nice if we could hear Him clearly. We find ourselves hoping for our own "burning bush" to point us in the right direction. Does God still speak to us today?

The answer is a resounding, "Yes! God does speak to us!" But sometimes we don't hear because we are listening for the wrong thing. There isn't always a clear and easy to understand answer, and most of us will never actually "hear" God's voice in our ears. But He speaks to us daily through our prayers, through Scripture, through our consciences and through the events He orchestrates to teach us and help us to grow spiritually.

Are you so busy listening for a voice in the night that you are missing opportunities to receive God's word in the world around you?

God's desire is for us to willingly wait until He is ready to reveal His Word, but we are often in a hurry, and may misinterpret or convince ourselves that He has told us something just because it is what we want to hear! Don't act in haste because you are tired of waiting for God to speak to you. Seek His counsel and wait for His instruction to guide you, otherwise you may miss out on God's finest and very best because you've taken a shortcut.

God speaks to us in many ways. He speaks through **His Word, our conscience, and the events around us.**

> *"Call to Me and I will answer you, and I will tell you great and mighty things, which you do not know."*
>
> *-Jeremiah 33:3*

The Bible is filled with God speaking His Word. This is literally the revealed Word of God, and is just as relevant today as it was thousands of years ago. God is eternal and so are His Words! They do not change with the passage of time, so if you want to hear Him speaking clearly, read His Word.

> *"All Scripture is God-created and is useful for teaching, rebuking, correcting and training in righteousness, so that the man of God may be thoroughly equipped for every good work."*
>
> *-2 Timothy 3:16-17*

Our conscience is one of the most profound ways that God speaks to us today. Think about it – whenever your conscience bothers you, isn't it because you've done something that is contrary to God's word? That is because God, in His infinite love for us, has given each of us a conscience that nudges our souls and tells us when we are wrong, gently guiding us back to the path God has laid out for us. He is the voice of love speaking inside our souls!

The challenges we face, the hardships we bear and the triumphs we experience are all part of God speaking to us. Through the circumstances we face each day, God is changing us and helping us to mature spiritually. As we draw closer to God, we will realize that He has been there all along.

But to truly hear God's Word, we must not look for ways to further our own agendas. We must be seeking *His will for us*. The more we seek after what God has planned for us, the more He will speak to us, whether through His Holy Word, through the voice of others, or through our consciences. We cannot expect revelation or demand that God speak to us – He will speak when the need is there, and if we are actively seeking Him, we will hear His words in our heart and soul. Sometimes He speaks to us quickly, other times we must wait quietly upon His word to be revealed in the time He knows is right and proper for us.

God promises in the Bible that He speaks through Christ and will speak to all who listen earnestly for His voice:

> *"Behold, I stand at the door and knock; if any man hear my voice, and open the door, I will come in to him."*
>
> *—Revelations 3:20*

Are you listening for God's word? Will you open the door and let Him in?

God Can Lead You to Self-Discovery

There are hundreds of self-help books on the shelves today about self-awareness or self-discovery. More people take time off every year from their normal lives so that they can "find themselves." In fact, it has even become somewhat of a joke that people going through a mid-life crisis are trying to find themselves – as though they misplaced who they are!

But it isn't always a joke. True self-discovery is crucial to being comfortable in our own skins and is a key element of being a successful Christian. God wants us to understand ourselves, not in a selfish way, but in the sense that we must understand our place in His creation and His plan if we are too be fully appreciative of Him. We can't know God without knowing ourselves, because we are His children!

Through the ages, many people have recognized this and prayed for the awareness to understand themselves better. St. Augustine asked God to guide him toward self-discovery centuries ago:

> *"Grant, Lord, that I may know myself that I may know Thee."*
>
> *–St. Augustine*

Self-discovery is about learning not only who you are, but what part you hold in God's plan. He didn't create you in order to simply take up space! He has a purpose especially for you, and until you go on the journey of self-discovery, you can't understand what your role is. After all, how can you fulfill the destiny God has for you unless you know what gifts you can use to achieve that destiny? Just as important is the flip side of self-discovery – awareness of your faults. Knowing what causes you to stumble and fall is crucial to success in any endeavor, but never more so than when you are seeking God.

> *"The unfolding of your words gives light; it imparts understanding to the simple."*
>
> *–Psalm 119:130*
>
> *"When you search for me, you will find me: if you seek me with all your heart."*
>
> *–Jeremiah 29:13*

So self-discovery goes both ways – God can help you achieve it, and the more self-aware you are, the closer you can draw to God. How wonderful that God has created this unique dynamic for us!

Ask God Questions to Discover Your True Self

God will always be there when we come to Him with questions. He wants us to ask questions so that He can give us the right answers and guide us in the right paths, so don't be afraid to ask when you're seeking your true self.

- Why am I here?
- What do you want me to do with my life?
- What do you want me to learn?
- How do I overcome my fears, self-doubts and insecurities?
- What steps do I need to take to further understand myself and God?

All of the questions above can be taken to God in prayer. Whenever you talk to God, you learn a bit more about yourself. You can discover ways to overcome your flaws when you lay them down before Him. You can understand better how to use the gifts He has given you and will be able to manage them better.

When you begin the journey of self-discovery through God, never be afraid of what you find out about yourself! God made you distinctive for a reason! Finding out what that reason is and following the plan God has for you is the greatest form of self-discovery there is !

God Can Heal Brokenness

You cannot change what you don't acknowledge or confront. When we are broken of spirit, the wounds of the past can overwhelm us and cause us pain and suffering, but God can heal our brokenness. He can't do this, however, if we don't first turn our hurts and sorrows over to Him.

There is nothing God hasn't heard before, nothing He hasn't seen. You can shed your tears and bring your heart aches to Him and He will heal your broken heart and wounded spirit. He understands your tears and will give you the grace to not only carry on, but to triumph, all you have to do is turn to Him with a contrite and willing heart. Ask God today to be the glue that binds the broken pieces of your shattered soul back together.

> *"He heals the brokenhearted and binds up their wounds."*
>
> *–Psalm 147:3*

How do we ask God to heal our brokenness? By making our wounded hearts and souls a living sacrifice to Him. Brokenness comes from holding on to our sorrows and letting them eat away at us. When we turn over those hurts to the Lord and ask Him to accept them, we have taken the first step toward healing.

> *"The sacrifices of God are a broken spirit: a broken and a contrite heart, O God, thou wilt not despise."*
>
> *–Psalm 51:17*

You must admit that you've turned away from Him to concentrate on your own pain, and put forth a contrite and loving heart. Ask the Lord sincerely to take away your selfishness and your inability to turn from your sorrow and pain, and He will give you the strength and love to move beyond your past and step into a loving future in His presence.

> *"Heal me, O Lord, and I shall be healed."*
>
> *–Jeremiah 17:14*

There is a straight and righteous path to God's healing if we know the steps to take:

Actively seek God and His healing.

Confess that you are broken and that you are in need of His healing power.

God Can Heal Brokenness

Forgive yourself and others for whatever has happened. As long as you hold onto blame or anger, your brokenness will remain.

Let go of the bitterness and acknowledge that, no matter what has befallen you, you have something to be thankful for. This can be the most difficult step, especially if your loss has been a profound one. But as you pray to the Lord, He will remind you of the amazing gift that He has given you – eternal life and His unending love! With these two great gifts, how can we hold onto our earthly sorrows?

Express your gratitude. Prayerfully thank the Lord for each day ahead of you that is a wealth of possibilities and the grace that grants you peace.

Remember that God has not burdened you with more than you can bear. You are still here! And with God's help you will rise from your knees with a stronger, steadier spirit than ever!

God will hear your entreaties and make good on His promise to you. He will bring joy and meaning back into your life.

> *"The Lord is near to all who call on Him, to all who call on Him in truth."*
>
> *–Psalm 145:18*

Five Great Needs Only God Can Fulfill

Everyone has human needs that go beyond the physical. If we have food, water, and shelter, we can survive. But to truly thrive, there are spiritual and emotional needs that we all have. We all strive to find ways to satisfy our need for *Love, Acceptance, Security, Identity* and *Purpose.* Some of us seek these in ourselves, in others and from society, but none of these needs can be truly fulfilled except by God.

Love

God's love is always present and unconditional. If you've ever had a friend or loved one that you felt you could trust completely, you've had a faint taste of what its like to be able to rely on someone without worry or fear. But even the strongest relationships can end, loved ones can die, circumstances can destroy our faith in others. Not so with God and His unconditional love because He is never-ending and never changing. Nothing in this world that you can do or say will alter His love for you. He will never leave you or forsake you. You can always, always find comfort and security through your relationship with God because it is, like Him, eternal.

No matter what you do, no matter how you look, no matter how many mistakes you've made, you can never let God down because He loves you without conditions, without measure and with no reservations or hidden agenda. God is guiding you through every experience of your life - not because you have earned it, but because God loves you no matter what. When the dark clouds settle and all others abandon you, the light of God will shine bright and show you the way. His guiding light is unconditional love.

> *"I trust in God's unfailing love forever and ever "*
> *—Psalm 52:8*
> *"For great is your steadfast love toward me"*
> *—Psalm 86:13*
> *"I am with you always to the end of the age"*
> *-Matthew 28:20*

Acceptance

From the time we are born, we search for acceptance. The sense of belonging to another person or to a group of people is a powerful affirmation. We try to please our parents as toddlers so that they will accept and love us. When we are in school, we hope to be accepted into the "popular crowd." At work, we want to be on the best project team or be accepted by our boss and coworkers. We enter into relationships because the other person accepts us.

But relationships fail, groups change over time and even our parents may be disappointed in our actions. The only true, unconditional acceptance is that offered by God. He loves us no matter what. He doesn't care what we look like or about the mistakes we've made. As His creation, He loves and accepts us unconditionally.

> *"To the praise of the glory of His grace, wherein*
> *He hath made us accepted in the Beloved."*
> *—Ephesians 1:6*

Security

There is such a sense of security that overwhelms us when we are safe in the arms of God. Although our circumstances can change from day to day, God is eternal. Many of us accumulate money and power, hoping these will keep us secure, but we can lose our money and our power so easily! The person who is on top today may be in the gutters tomorrow. No power we gain for ourselves can protect us from the many possible problems of this world.

God, however, is our eternal protection. He is our security and shelter in any storm because He will not leave us in times of trouble. No matter what happens, He will guard our souls and direct our footsteps if we ask Him to. Let yourself be secure in God's abiding presence and you will always feel safe.

"You will be protected and take your rest in safety."
—Job 11:18

"Never will I leave, never will I forsake you."
—Hebrews 13:5

Identity

Do you put on a mask for others so that they will see you in a particular way? Do you have different identities for different people? We are always trying to define ourselves in relation to other people. Are you a mother? Employee? The best friend? The fun one? Our identities are often tied to what we can provide to others, and it can be difficult to be all things to all people.

God knows our true identity – the one that is whole and complete, the hidden most part of our heart and soul. We are uniquely, fearfully and marvelously made children of God! When we discover the power and presence of God within ourselves, we have found our true identity, one that doesn't depend on what others see. We are, and always will be, unique creations of the Master Creator.

"I am a member of God's household"
—Ephesians 2:19

"I am God's child."
—John 1:12

Purpose

We all wonder why we are here occasionally. Do we have a purpose to fulfill? Is being a parent our ultimate role? Are we supposed to be achieving great things at work? Do we have a destiny to fulfill? We can spend our lives worrying about what our purpose is, but it will be an exercise in futility unless we turn to God for guidance. No one on earth knows what you *should* be doing.

God decides our life's plan and purpose here on earth. He created you to fulfill a divine purpose, no matter how large or small, that is part of His eternal plan. Isn't it reassuring to know that what you do and say matters in the grand scheme of things? Our purpose is essential!

> *"The Lord will fulfill His purpose for me."*
> *-Psalm 138:8*

Tonight as you say your prayers, thank the Lord for providing everything you need and all that your heart desires, including unconditional love and acceptance, unfailing security, a unique identity and a true purpose!

The Power of God

The power of God is unlimited and, in its vastness, unknowable in all its forms, yet this amazing and vast power gives us hope and should give us the confidence to go forward in life without fear. Think about the infinite power of God – He is the One who rolls back the clouds and brings forth sunshine after a storm. He orders the winds to blow and creates the seasons in order to bring forth food on the earth and provide for all the creatures on it. We can rely on the fact that night follows day and winter is followed by spring because God's power makes it so.

In fact, God is unique in all the universe in His power. He has attributes that no one and nothing else has that demonstrate the infinite variety and omniscience of His power:

- No other creature is capable of creation from nothing. God alone created the universe itself and all the creatures in it. He created night and day, the planets and stars and everything on the earth that sustains life. He willed the very universe into existence and existed before it came into being.

- No other creature is self-sustaining like God is. Plants require water and light, animals and people require food. God requires nothing – He simply Is, with nothing else required.

- No other creature can forgive like God can forgive. While we can forgive others for harm they may have done to us, no one has the ability to forgive us all of our transgressions and grant absolution – giving us hope of eternal life.

- No other creature is Infinite. He was here at the beginning of time, and is outside of time. In fact, God and His son, Jesus Christ, *are* the beginning and the end, the Alpha and Omega of the universe.

"In the beginning was the Word, and the Word was with God, and the Word was God. He was with God in the beginning. Through Him all things were made. In Him was life, and that life was the light of men."

–John 1:1-4

So who or what should we put our faith in? The power of kingdoms and men will fade away, but God is eternal. He is like nothing and no one else and can be relied on for all your needs. Do you fully realize and understand the power of His presence in your life? Many believers speak of the acts of God, but have you ever considered the amazing power of His presence in your own life, the personal power that you have by giving your life over to Him?

"If God is for us, who can be against us?"
—Roman 8:31

The next time you are fearful or do not know where to turn, remember that the most powerful force on earth and in heaven is God. He doesn't have to do anything but be there, and you have all you need to overcome anything.

"For nothing will be impossible with God."
—Luke 1:37

Understanding the Will of God

*"I can of myself do nothing...because I do not seek
my own but the will of the Father who sent me."*
–John 5:30

It is easy for others to tell us that we should "do God's will," but it is difficult for most of us to understand what God's will for our lives truly is. Angels don't often land in our front yards with trumpet fanfare to announce what we should be doing (although that would be wonderful, wouldn't it?). In today's world, it can be difficult to know the will of God because we have so many others demanding our time and trying to tell us what to do. Sometimes the most difficult obstacles are our own wants and desires, which may be at odds with God's will.

So how do we discover God's will in for us? We must *pray earnestly, understand our circumstances* and remember to *study God's word.* The Bible is full of references to God's will for all of us. If we study the word of God and follow them, we are heading in the right direction. Fortunately, all we have to do is read the Scriptures to find clear instructions:

> *"He hath showed thee, O man, what is good; and what doth the Lord require of thee, but to do justly, and to love mercy, and to walk humbly with thy God."*
>
> *–Micah 6:8*

Micah clearly tells us what God's will is for every one of us – mercy, justice and humbleness before the Lord. He desires this for all of mankind. It's interesting that most of us know instinctively that we should be merciful, kind, just, honest and faithful. These principles of fairness and care are nearly universal and we know in our heart of hearts that they are God's will.

The difficulty is that often fulfilling God's will can cause conflict in our lives. Sometimes it's easier to just do what we think will be easiest or best for us, forgetting about God and the people around us. We may tell ourselves that we can't always keep all of God's commandments, or that it's hard to understand what true justice is, or even that honesty may not always be in our best interests.

We would be so wrong! Because God's will is always for our lives to be prosperous, fulfilled and righteous. Perhaps it is easier if we look at Jesus' answer regarding God's will. He explains what the greatest commandment is – and even if we forget *every other commandment or instruction of God* – if we follow God's will in this, everything else will naturally follow!

> *"'Teacher, which is the great commandment in the Law?' And He said to them, 'You shall love the Lord your God with all your heart, and with all your soul, and with all your mind. This is the great and foremost commandment. The second is like it, "You shall love your neighbor as yourself."'*
> —Matthew 22:36-39

Think about this. If we love God with all of our hearts, minds and souls, then we will naturally seek justice, be humble and live righteously in order to praise Him. If we love our neighbors as ourselves, we will be honest, fair and just in everything we do.

God's will is also expressed in Romans:

> *"And do not be conformed to this world, but be transformed by the renewing of your mind, that you may prove what it is the **good** and **acceptable** and **perfect** will of God."*
> —Romans 12:2

Any time you have a difficult choice before you, simply ask yourself these questions:

- Is this **a good** thing to do for all concerned?
- Is this **acceptable to God**?
- Is this God's **perfect** will? (Does it meet Biblical standards?)

To find the answer to these questions, pray earnestly for guidance, read the Scriptures and listen to that part of your heart that is honest and just, not concerned with you and your desires, but dedicated to God.

> *"Seek His will in all you do, and He will direct your paths."*
>
> *—Proverbs 3:6*

Are you ready to seek, accept and understand the will of God? Then bow your head and pray for Him to reveal His individual will for your life. So long as you seek, you will find what you need to fulfill God's will. The safest place we can ever be is in the *will* of God.

God Works On Our Insides First

Most of us think that if we could just get a better job, meet the right person, buy that gorgeous house…or something else we're longing for, we will be happy. We think that once we've achieved some concrete goal or obtained a certain amount of money, we will be happy; but we can be very disappointed when we find out that the recognition or the money don't give us the happiness we wanted.

The circumstances you are in aren't nearly as important as how you *respond* to those circumstances. If you respond with prayer and a sincere desire to love Him and your fellow man despite bad circumstances, you will discover that God gives you the skills you need to overcome your circumstances or be happy *despite* them. Trusting in God, opening yourself up to possibilities and giving of yourself to others will lead to true happiness. God's love and love for yourself (which naturally lead to happiness) are perfected in loving others. He's made it easy for us to find happiness by trying to make others happy. What a wonderful plan – we increase our joy by bringing joy to others!

> *"So I concluded that there is nothing better for people than to be happy and to enjoy themselves as long as they can."*
>
> *–Ecclesiastes 3:12*

God understands that the material things and the adulation of others isn't what will make us happy. That's why He doesn't always grant our wishes right away. He's working on our insides first because He knows that what matters is what is in our heart and soul. God focuses on the real source of happiness – our relationship with Him – so that we will be happy with ourselves and ready to handle the good and the bad that life hands us.

Are you happy with yourself? If not, no amount of money and no change in your circumstances will change things. You have to learn to *love yourself like God loves you.* When you can do this, you will be happy within your own skin, and the rest of your life will fall into place more easily. Turn yourself over to God body, heart and soul and you will be amazed – He never leaves us the way He found us! He is always working on us, healing old wounds and restoring our faith. As He does this, you will find yourself increasingly seeking to do what is right and good in His eyes – and you'll discover the joy of a Christian life.

God Works On Our Insides First

> *"It is God who produces in you the desires and actions that please Him."*
>
> *—Philippians 2:13*

Begin working today on getting to know and love God and you will soon know yourself better, love yourself and understand yourself. Allow God to work on your insides and you will be healed of the disappointments and hurt in your life – and room will open up in your soul for true happiness. Ask God to work on you from the inside out so that you will become the person God has always meant you to be and you will find happiness in His purpose for you. Give God control and let Him mold you as He sees fit. Surrender yourself and find happiness in God's plan.

> *"'For I know the plans I have for you,' declares the Lord, 'plans to prosper you and not to harm you, plans to give you hope and a future.'"*
>
> *—Jeremiah 29:11*

Having an Attitude of Gratitude

As you read this chapter, take a moment to answer the following question, "Is there a reason for me to be thankful today?" If you are alive to read the question, then you have a reason for rejoicing! It may not always seem that way when troubles press in on you, but as long as you are alive, you have the opportunity to change your life and move forward.

One of the most important gifts of all is life, and it was given to you by the Lord. Sometimes we forget the generosity of a loving God. After all, He doesn't need us and did not have to create us in the first place. Yet He wished to share His blessings and so created man in His own image so that He could shower man with love. And even when man first betrayed God in the Garden of Eden, God continued to love and protect mankind. He forgave us our faults and sent His only son, Jesus Christ, to give us guidance and grant us forgiveness! And God continues to do this, even though we often forget to be grateful for His kindness.

Now think back over the previous month. Have you lived in Gratitude? Have you remembered and acknowledged God's grace and goodwill in your life? It's easy to forget our many blessings when we are stressed, but we need to re-evaluate our lives during these moments. When your job stresses you, thank God that you are employed. When your children talk back, praise God for giving you healthy children. Even when you are going through a painful separation or quarrel, remember that God is there for you, and be thankful that He is there to pull you through.

> *"And let the peace of Christ rule in your hearts, to which indeed you were called in the one body. And be thankful."*
>
> *–Colossians 3:15*

When we have an attitude of gratitude, we soon discover that we attract greater good in our lives. Be grateful for all of the good that the Lord has granted you, and you will soon reap even greater blessings. As you read this article, be grateful for the gift of sight and the opportunity you had to learn to read and learn. Giving thanks to God for all of the many daily blessings in your life – shelter, food, your senses, friends and family – opens your heart to all the good you have and enables you to appreciate and share your blessings. Sharing those blessings and being grateful for them brings you closer to God.

> *"Yours, O Lord, is the greatness and power and the glory and majesty and the splendor,*

Having an Attitude of Gratitude

for everything in heaven and earth is yours…
In your hands are strength and power
To exalt and give strength to all.
Now, our God, we give you thanks,
And praise your glorious name."
—1 Chronicles 29:11-13

So as you move through your days and weeks, keep your eyes on the goodness of God and recognize that He has, in His generosity and love, given you far more than anyone else can ever give you. Find the blessings in every situation and you will develop an attitude of gratitude for the many physical, material, emotional and spiritual blessings that have been given by God, the source of all good in our lives. Each day, show your gratitude to God and thank Him with all your heart.

"And whatever you do, in word or deed, do
everything in the name of the Lord Jesus, giving
thanks to God the Father through Him."
—Colossians 3:17

The Power of Our Testimony

In a courtroom, testimony is given by witnesses. Those witnesses tell the story of what happened and what they know as they experienced it. They tell a story that they believe is true, and they testify in order to help others understand what happened. As Christians, we have a testimony of our own to give – the story of the power of God's love and the miracles He has worked in your lives.

But how many of us actually take the time to witness to others? When is the last time you gave your testimony about God's presence in your life? You should tell your story whenever the opportunity presents itself because it will give God the Glory He deserves and it will encourage and inspire those who hear it.

The power of individual testimony shouldn't be underestimated. If a friend or co-worker is having a rough time, take the time to listen and give them a shoulder to cry on. But don't stop there – let them know you are praying for them and that God loves them. When others see that your life is blessed by confidence, love and God's presence, they will want to know more.

You can give your testimony a number of ways. You can tell your story, dividing it into "BC," for Before Christ's presence and "AC," for after Christ entered your life. Reveal your feelings of hopelessness and loneliness before Christ entered your heart, then talk about the fulfillment, strength and sense of purpose you've discovered with God.

Think back on what you have shared with your friends and family in the past months. Have you told others about a good book you enjoyed? A great movie that you encourage them to see? How often have you talked about your relationship with God? Probably not much, which is a shame. After all, we know what is important in someone's life by what they talk about.

Your uncle talks constantly about his passion for vintage cars, your best friend talks a lot about her fiancé, and your sister loves chatting about shopping. Yet how often do we talk about the God we love and who loves us? If you love God, talk about Him! Share the good news with others around you!

Every time we testify to God's grace and love, we are opening up an opportunity for others to discover God. And with God's love bringing us joy and peace, we are increasing our own happiness by sharing it. Showing God's love to others is contagious – the more we share, the more others will receive and it will be passed on. What a wonderful way to praise the Lord! Let your light as God's child shine in both word and deed.

> *"You are the light of the world. A city on a hill cannot be hidden. Neither do people light a lamp and put it under a bowl. Instead they put it on a stand and it gives light to everyone in the house. In the same way, let your light shine before men, that they may see your good deeds and praise your Father in heaven."*
> —Matthew 5:13-16

So the next time you are talking to others about what is important in your life, don't forget to give God the glory He deserves. You will not only please Him, you may open a door for someone else to explore the Lord's blessings. The power of your testimony may be what brings a lost and hurting soul to God. There is no greater thanks you can give Him than this, because He's seeking his lost sheep even today.

> *"I have other sheep who are not of this sheep pen. I must bring them also. They too will hear my voice, and there shall be one flock and one shepherd."*
> —John 10:16

Wouldn't you like to be a Christian who brings new sheep to our Shepherd? Then take every opportunity to testify to the power of God's love!

Writing a Heartfelt Letter to God-Finding Emotional Freedom

When there is no closure in our lives, we continue to hurt long after the moment that first caused us pain has passed. When we are troubled by past transgressions we can't forget, our lives continue to be an open wound that can't heal. We become "walking wounded" and can't get on with our lives. We feel incomplete and unfinished, as though something in our lives is lacking.

How do you find closure after death, separation, divorce, or the pain of a parent who doesn't love you? What do you do to find peace when your life continues to show the scars of past abuse or terrible loss?

God will soothe your soul and help bring you peace if only you will lay your sorrows and anger at His feet. Sometimes it's hard to go to the Lord and confess how angry we are at a loved one because of a past slight or some terrible harm they caused us. After all, we want to be good Christians and forgive – but if there is still pain in our hearts, it can be difficult to do.

Write Your Unresolved Pain Down

It may help if you try writing a letter to God. Writing down what is eating at your soul can help you move past it. We hate to rant and rave at God when we pray, shouting about how bitter or disappointed we are; it seems so disrespectful. But God *wants* to hear everything in our hearts – even the ugly stuff. So sit down tonight and write a letter to God. It might look like this:

> *"Dear God,*
>
> *I'm so angry! I hate my sister for betraying me, and I can't get past it. I wish she would just go away and leave me alone forever….."*

Once you start writing, you will find that all of the bitterness, hurt and sorrow will come spilling out and onto the page. That's good! It's very cleansing to finally admit, even to yourself, that you have been hanging on to unfinished business and letting yourself dwell on the past.

After you've written your letter, make it a sacrifice to God, for even our pain, when given with a true and faithful heart, is a gift to our Lord. He will take the sorrow you've written about and soothe it away for you. Some people may even want to burn the letter after they've asked God to help them find closure. It is a simple ritual that can give you a feeling of release

– you have admitted what the problem is, asked God to help you move forward, and now you can let it go!

> *"Heal me, O Lord, and I shall be healed."*
> *—Jeremiah 17:14*

Once you've done this, you will feel a sense of peace as the closure you've been seeking for so long finds its place in your heart!

God is a Healer

*"Then your light shall break forth like the dawn,
and healing shall spring up quickly."*
                                               –Isaiah 58:8

When someone you love is sick or when you are sick, you should pray for God's healing power to wash over you. This doesn't mean that you shouldn't see a doctor or take full advantage of all of the opportunities that medical science has to offer. I don't recommend abandoning medical or surgical treatments and using *only* prayer; I feel that a complimentary approach is best. The combination of medicine and prayer can be very powerful and I think a lot of people today misunderstand and think that we can't use both.

Through prayer, we acknowledge that there is a greater wisdom and higher power than anything on earth. We get in touch with that power and ask that God bring miracles and His love into our lives, but we don't have to turn our backs on the rich and varied medical traditions available here on earth when we do pray, because God heals in many ways:

God heals through doctors and nurses. He has given these professionals their God-given talents and abilities so that, through them, He can touch the lives of people every day in millions of ways both great and small. It is one of the main reasons He creates each of us with unique talents and interests - so that each of us can become someone special and unique who will touch others and, in some cases, *heal* others.

So when we pray, we should pray that God will guide the hearts and hands of the doctors, nurses and surgeons who are taking care of our love ones or ourselves.

God can perform miracles of healing. Although we may find it difficult to ask for a miracle, God rejoices in our faith when we believe that He can cure the hopelessly sick and He sometimes does perform miracles. Ask and don't be afraid - God listens to our prayers.

God heals by providing comfort and strength. Not every patient recovers and not everyone is healed; that is what we sometimes find most unfathomable about God's ways. While many people recover from an illness, some do not. But the power of prayer is amazing! Even doctors and researchers have confirmed that people who pray feel less pain and are stronger and more at peace than those who don't. Perhaps we need to look at the power of prayer in this light - God heals us not only when He heals our illness, but when He touches us to take away the hurt and bring us spiritual comfort and ease.

His love touches us not only physically but spiritually and emotionally.

Remember that God is the supreme healer and pray for His intercession:

Let Us Pray

Dear Heavenly Father,

You are my help in every need and sustainer. I know that nothing is too hard for you.

Heavenly Father, I am praying and believing now for the complete healing and restoration of (fill-in-the-blank with your health concerns).

Grant me the peace, strength and faith to endure each and every day. Guide the hearts, hands and minds of those that are caring for me.

I place my complete trust in you, Father.

Knowing my oneness with you, Heavenly Father, I experience true healing.

Thank you, Lord, for sending your word and your healing power.

In Jesus Name, Amen.

With absolute faith and trust in God, we affirm oneness with the mighty healing power of God. Thank You, God, for healing us in every needed way. We are healthy and strong because of our Heavenly Father.

How to Overcome Grief

Grief is a part of the healing process when you have experienced any kind of loss. Getting past that grief, whether it is over the loss of a loved one, a relationship or a job, and moving on with your life may leave you feeling like a stranger in a strange land. The familiar may seem unfamiliar and the routine may become a challenge when you are filtering everything through the haze of sorrow and confusion brought on by grief.

You need to keep in mind that even during your moments of greatest sorrow, you are not alone. Remember that you are eternally in the presence of God's divine love, which fills any void temporarily left by grief.

> *"This is my comfort in my distress, that your promises give me life."*
>
> *–Psalm 119:50*

There are experts who break down the stages of grief into five categories. These can be very helpful when defining the various phases you go through as you adjust to traumatic events in your life:

- Stage One: Denial
- Stage Two: Pain
- Stage Three: Anger
- Stage Four: Depression
- Stage Five: Acceptance

While these five stages are an excellent way to gauge whether you are moving forward, there is another way to look at grief and how you handle it – a three-part process of *meeting it, managing it* and *mastering it.* These three phases allow you to process your grief in your life in clear, straight-forward ways that enable you to move forward with God's help.

Meeting Your Grief

Meeting your grief is the process of letting it in and acknowledging it. You need to get past the denial that you may go through in the early stages after something tragic has occurred. You can't cope properly with sorrow unless you are able to face it head-on, accepting it for what it is and how it is impacting your life.

Praying for God's help as you face your grief will give you the strength to accept the loss and understand that you have the strength with His love to survive that loss. There are many different kinds of loss that can be a source of grief. Regardless of what they are, you must be able to meet them and look them square in the face and be able to embrace it, if not willingly, at least realistically.

Sometimes we deny losses in our lives for many months or even years rather than meeting them and acknowledging them. Examples of loss like this include: loss of trust, loss of love, marriage or a spouse, loss of virginity, loss of security, loss of acceptance, loss of friendship, loss of innocence, loss of education, loss of security, loss of a child or loss of employment.

When you are ready to let go of the festering pain that these losses are causing you, pray to the Lord and He will help you Meet Your Grief. You will need to take that time to properly mourn. You may cry for a while, or spend some time alone or talk with someone who understands your pain. Whatever you need to do to allow the pain to be washed away is fine. At that point, you have taken the first step toward overcoming your grief.

Managing Your Grief

Managing your grief means understanding how to live your life and move forward with grief as a part of the whole. The Lord will give you the strength to integrate your sorrow into your daily living and learn how to slowly overcome the pain and depression that may have stopped you from moving forward before you met your grief. Management is about being able to slowly let the normalcy of life back into your days and giving yourself permission to move on. When your life begins to feel familiar to you once again, you are successfully managing your grief.

Mastering Your Grief

Mastering your grief is when you are able to move past it and overcome it. You do not have to forget the past or lose the memories of what has happened, but you *do* have to overcome the power that the grief has to hurt you. It is healthy to grieve a loss, but there comes a time for the mourning to end and new life to begin.

Mastering your grief can be difficult because you may feel guilty moving on, but God assures us that our lives are meant to have many different phases and nothing, including grief, is meant to last forever. He has created a world for us that is meant to be celebrated even when bad things happen.

> *"There is a time for everything, and a season for every activity under heaven…*
> *a time to weep and a time to laugh, a time to mourn and a time to dance".*
>
> *–Ecclesiastes 3:1-4*

When you have a grief to cope with, remember that the Lord is always listening and will be there to give you comfort and support. Pray for His help and you will find that the road toward meeting, managing and mastering your grief will be one you can travel with less sorrow than you would have expected.

The indwelling love of God is our source of inspiration for overcoming grief. Thank You, God, for Your presence of love, life, and light.

God Uses Ordinary People to Do Extraordinary Things

There is no such thing as the wrong side of the tracks with God. I think it was Jim Collins who wrote the book "Good to Great," which said, "It is a sin to be good when you can be great." The power of God is unlimited. God is not limited in any way by your education, economic status, race or social standing. Those are artificial limitations that only matter to the world, not to the Lord.

If you say, "God, I am available to You and I submit and surrender to Your will for my life," something amazing will start to happen in your life because God will use you to do His will and purpose. God will take the ordinary and turn it into the extraordinary! Develop a habit of being what God knows you can be and surrender fully to His will. Remember that His view is the long view of the world and His goals are not focused on the little picture. God can do extraordinary things using ordinary people in seemingly small ways.

There was a young girl at the turn of the century outside of Philadelphia who was crying near a small church when the pastor walked by. When he asked her what was wrong, she sobbed that there hadn't been enough room in the Sunday School class for her. Seeing her filthy clothes, the pastor guessed that she may have been turned away for other reasons. He marched her back in and found a place for her in the class. She listened and loved the Bible stories she heard each Sunday after that.

Two years later, the little girl died. When the pastor came to make final arrangements, he discovered a coin purse with her belongings. Inside the coin purse was 57 cents and a slip of paper that said, "To make the church bigger so more kids can go to the Sunday School."

The pastor told the girl's story that Sunday in church, and challenged his deacons to raise enough money to build a bigger church. The newspapers picked up the story. And a realtor offered a parcel of land worth thousands of dollars to build the church on. When told that the church couldn't afford the asking price, he offered to sell it to them for 57 cents.

It would seem impossible to build a church with 57 cents, but that didn't stop one little girl from trying to create a miracle. Today you can go to Temple Baptist church of Philadelphia and Temple University. Go visit the Sunday School building next to Good Samaritan Hospital, where there is more than enough room for everyone. In one room you will see the picture of a young girl who started it all with 57 cents. Alongside it is the picture of the Reverend Dr. Russell Conwell, who multiplied that 57 cents through countless others.

God had taken the very ordinary donation of a poor child, less than a dollar, and turned it into something extraordinary! It became the driving force that turned the heart of a landowner, motivated the revival of a church and eventually founded a University! All because an ordinary young minister made sure an ordinary young girl went to Sunday School one ordinary morning.

> *"I can do all things through Him who strengthens me."*
>
> *–Philippians 4:13*

God always sees what is inside of us. We all have gifts, talents and opportunities that He can shape into miraculous moments. We must stop looking at what we don't have and start looking at what God can do in our lives.

Rejection is God's Protection

Right now you're probably thinking, "Wait a minute, that doesn't sound right. How can rejection be a form of protection?" But I'm not talking about rejecting by God. The Lord will *never* reject you – He will always love and accept you! The rejection I'm talking about is the rejection you sometimes face in your own life. When you feel like the world is rejecting you, whether at work, in your personal life or through the loss of something important to you, that may be God's way of protecting you.

No matter where you are, you should accept it as the place God wants you to be and trust in God's perfect timing. Thank God that He has seen in His wisdom to answer some of your prayers in unexpected ways and to answer others in the negative, because sometimes what we thought was the best for us wasn't the best at all.

> *"Sometimes I thank God for unanswered prayers*
> *Remember when you're talkin' to the man upstairs*
> *That just because he doesn't answer doesn't mean he don't care*

Some of God's greatest gifts are unanswered prayers"

—Garth Brooks Song

The song lyrics above are good ones to keep in mind. We should thank the Lord for all of the doors that He has opened and thank Him even more for the doors that He has closed in our lives. We should learn to trust that He know what is best for us and is in control of our destinies. We may not understand everything that is happening and we don't know what is in store for us in the future, but if we trust in Him, we can move forward knowing that He has our best interests at heart. After all, He knows the future and understands that there may be something far greater just around the next corner for us.

When we lose a job, go through a divorce, don't get that promotion we wanted or face any other form of rejection or disappointment, we must remember to fight our discouragement and put our faith in God. The temporary rejection is God's protection of our future. He is protecting us from some future hurt or sorrow by putting us on the proper path in the here and now. Yes, it can be a painful and harsh path to walk, but if we walk it in faith and allow God to comfort and keep us, we will get through the rejection and we will come out stronger on the other side, ready to accept the greater gifts He has waiting for us in the future!

Rejection is God's Protection

Relax and learn to trust God. He is on your side. Ask God for His will and not your own. Being in God's will is the safest place you can ever be. One of the most important aspect of faith is trusting that God will know what is right for you, even when you don't understand His reasons. When it seems like your prayers aren't being answered, it may be that God is protecting you from danger or sorrow that you can't see, the timing isn't right or that God has something far better planned for you that you haven't even thought about. Give yourself over to Him completely and realize that any rejection you suffer from is only temporary here on earth, and that God's plan is all-encompassing and will always prevail.

> *"Trust in the Lord with all your heart and do not rely on your own insight."*
>
> *–Proverbs 3:5*
>
> *"Seek His will in all you do and He will direct your paths."*
>
> *-Proverbs 3:6*

How to Be Happy

Wouldn't it be nice if there was an easy way to guarantee happiness? So many of us find ourselves thinking, "If only I had a decent job/special someone/more money I would be happy. Unfortunately, once we get the thing we've most desired, we often find that the happiness we thought it would bring doesn't appear.

That's because happiness comes from the *inside,* not something external. No one can "make" us happy. It comes from being comfortable with who you are and understanding and embracing the choices we make in life. Are you content with who you are becoming? Happiness is an inside job. It is a choice and a way of life.

Many people waste their lives in the pursuit of happiness drinking, using drugs and pursuing money or relationships that are outside of God' law. They soon find that these are simply temporary band-aids, not genuine paths to happiness. They might temporarily cover up your unhappiness, but they won't lead to lasting joy. Perhaps true happiness means something more than living in the moment!

> *"Happy is the man that findeth wisdom and the man that getteth understanding."*
>
> *–Proverbs 3:13*

> *"Where there is no vision, the people perish: but he that keepeth the law, happy is he."*
>
> *–Proverbs 29:18*

The two scriptures above give us some powerful advice on happiness. They tell us that if we choose to seek wisdom and understanding and follow God's law, we will find happiness. Think about that – we need to seek to understand God's world better and follow the rules He has set for us in order to find happiness. But that makes it simpler, doesn't it? After all the Bible IS God's law and is full of his wisdom. As Christians, we have the "instruction manual" for happiness right at our fingertips!

We are poor judges of what will make us happy. Our lives without God are proof of that. Divorce, depression, loss of self-esteem, anger at those around us….All of these run rampant on our lives without God. Why? Because we chased after what we *thought* would make us happy! But if we follow God's path, putting our trust in Him, we will discover happiness right on our doorstep.

How to Be Happy

"Happy is he that hath the God of Jacob for his help, whose hope is in the Lord his God."

–Psalms 146:5

With the Lord's help, obstacles are overcome and we find peace that surpasses earthly goods, success or even finding that "special someone." How does this happen? What is so wonderful about being a Christian and dedicating our lives to God?

The ultimate promise given to us by God through Jesus Christ makes every day we live a blessed one. What promise does God give us that is so joyful? He has told us that ***the best is yet to come!*** Yes, our lives on this earth can be happy and filled with God's purpose, but nothing can compare to what we, as Christians, will inherit in the next life.

Eternal Life Everlasting, seated with God and His angels, is the ultimate happiness, and as Christians we are all entitled to this amazing inheritance! How can we *not* be happy, knowing what is in store for us as Children of God?

"For God so loved the world, that He gave His only begotten Son, that whosoever believeth in Him should not perish, but have everlasting life."

–John 3:16

If we truly believe in God's love and mercy, with such a glorious promise before us, how can we ever be anything but happy?

How to Reach Your Divine Potential

"Your belief, obedience and faith in God can produce any future you want in life"
—Robert Moment

It's natural to want to achieve success in life. Although we can glory in what is promised for our future in God's eternal life, we do have to live in this world for a time, and it is human nature to want our lives in the here and now to be pleasant. Does the Bible have anything to say about achieving goals and reaching our true potential in life? Yes!

"This book of the law shall not depart out of thy mouth; but thou shalt meditate therein day and night, that thou mayest observe to do according to all that is written therein: for then thou shalt make thy way prosperous, and then shalt thou have good success."

-Joshua 1:8

The above passage is telling you what you need to do to reach your full potential – you must take the time to learn and apply the teachings of the Lord. Only this will lead to success in your life. Jesus' teachings also allude to how our way of life can help us achieve our potential. He and His disciples remind us in the New Testament that faith in God will help us to become great.

> *"But seek ye first the kingdom of God, and His righteousness; and all these things shall be added unto you."*
>
> *–Matthew 6:33*

Why does God want us to prosper? Because He is the one that created each and every one of us, and within us He planted the seed of potential. This divine gift from God has been entrusted to us. We must care for it so that we can help it grow and thrive in this world, nourished by God's word and basking in the light of His love.

You are special – a child of God! Don't we always want what is best for our children? How much more does God want for His children whom He loves? By honoring and obeying our heavenly Father, we gain insight and guidance that will lead us to achieve our potential, which makes our God exalt in our successes.

Of course, God does allow us to face adversity, both personal and financial, in order to help us to grow strong and faithful. From our trials we learn valuable lessons. The end result is that we become stronger, more faithful children who are able and worthy of success. If we did not learn, we would squander our potential.

God watches over us, protects us, and expects us to have worthy goals. We can ask Him to help us achieve what we want, but only if we *know* what we want – what our *goals are.* God will bless us with what we desire if we focus on our goals and look at them through the lens of His love, praying specifically for His help in pursuing our goals.

> *"If ye abide in me, and my words abide in you, he shall ask what ye will, and it shall be done unto you."*
>
> *–John 15:7*

In order to "ask what we will," we must have goals so that we know what to ask for. If we follow His laws and ask in full awareness of what are goals should be, God will give us whatever it takes to reach our full potential!

> *"You shall be successful."*
>
> *-Joshua 1:8*

Continue to strive to reach your potential, keeping in mind, "I am a child of God, blessed with unlimited talents and abilities. Through Him, I will reach my potential and become a successful child of the Lord."

Caregivers are God's Precious Gift to Us

Caregivers are unique and special people and are a precious gift from the Lord. They nurture others, provide solace during times of pain or turmoil, and help to shape our lives. They provide great comfort, healing and understanding to those who need tenderness, attention and love. In fact, caregivers are reflections of God in their example of sacrifice for others.

If you are a caregiver, you know that sometimes it can weight you down and wear away at your energy and mood. But take heart in knowing that you are doing God's work here on earth. The good you do for others will come full circle, bringing you blessings in unexpected ways and from different people. Sometimes it may seem that those blessings are in the distance, but rest easy knowing that God sees and loves your care for others because it is what He has commanded us to do:

"In everything do to others what you would have them do to you; for this is the law of the prophets."
—Matthew 7:12

Being a caregiver is about putting others before yourself; something that isn't always easy. We are so tied to the earthly concept of taking care of ourselves and looking out for our own benefit that it can seem unfair to have to take care of others, particularly if there are problems the person we're caring for brought on themselves. But God doesn't differentiate between people that way – He loves the sinner as well as the saint, and desires that we care for all people as His people.

When you feel like you are being dragged down by your responsibilities as a caregiver, remember that you are imitating Christ when you show humility and service to others. These are the ideals of Christian living in action, and God will provide you comfort, even as you comfort others. He will give you the strength you need to carry on and will not forget that you have lived in His image.

Caregivers often develop a special relationship with the Lord through their service. Humbling yourself to the needs of others can bring you great spiritual insight – you realize the greatness of the sacrifice made for you through Christ, you understand the overwhelming love of the Lord, and you prepare yourself for heaven by bringing yourself closer to God's ideal for all of us.

There is a traditional and much-loved hymn that demonstrates the soul of a caregiver. The words express that attitude that God hopes each of us will have when confronted with someone's need for a caregiver:

Caregivers are God's Precious Gift to Us

"I, who made the stars of night,
I will make their darkness bright.
Who will bear my light to them?
Whom shall I send?

Here am I, Lord. Is it I, Lord?
I have heard you calling in the night.
I will go, Lord, if you lead me.
I will hold your people in my heart."

Answer God's call to you when a caregiver is needed, and become one of His precious gifts to the world. Your heart and soul will profit far more from your service than anything that you could ever lose.

"Finally, all of you, have unity of spirit, sympathy, love for one another, a tender heart, and a humble mind."

–1 Peter 3:8

How to Forgive Yourself

Many of us have felt the uplifting power of forgiving someone else; however, many people have a difficult time with self-blame and guilt, which makes it a struggle to forgive themselves. For instance, many people struggle with the guilt and self-blame associated with a divorce or even the death of a loved one. The reality is that you cannot heal and move forward after a personally devastating event if you are unable to forgive yourself.

To move forward in life, you need to release the pain, hurt, and guilt. Loving and forgiving yourself is the best gift you can give yourself. To receive this special and meaningful gift of forgiveness, you have to be ready to move forward and you have to want to free yourself of the guilt and blame. If you are, you must forgive yourself for the mistakes you have made in the past. Forgiving yourself can be a difficult challenge because the darkness is masking the light. It is easy to try to avoid thinking about your mistakes, but the negativity can be powerful and eat away at your self-confidence and self-esteem. You may start to wonder if you are really worthy of not only the love of others, but also God's love. It is essential to your spiritual and emotional health to forgive yourself just as God forgives you. And He does forgive you, completely, and with no reservations!

> *"You are a God ready to forgive, gracious and merciful."*
>
> *—Nehemiah 9:17*
>
> *"Do not judge, and you will not be judged; do not condemn, and you will not be condemned. Forgive, and you will be forgiven."*
>
> *—Luke 6:37*

When you are ready to forgive yourself, there are six steps that I have found very helpful in helping me on the path to self-forgiveness. I hope they will help you in your struggle to let go of your past mistakes and embrace forgiveness:

Steps to Forgiving Yourself

1. **Get a sheet of paper and a pen or pencil.** At the top of the paper, write down your name. Now, relax and think about the events in your past that brings out feelings of guilt and shame. These are experiences that you have never been able to let go of and have not forgiven yourself for.

2. **Write down your past wrongdoings and the people that you hurt and how you hurt them.** Was it physical or verbal abuse? Deceit? Neglecting someone important to you?

Unfaithfulness? Addiction? Cheating on a Spouse? Rejection? Theft? Dishonesty? Trickery? Financial? Other wrongdoing? Writing is helpful because you put your wrongdoings and thoughts in sentences. As a result, your mind will be able to process your thought more clearly and you will gain a fresh perspective and deeper understanding about your past mistakes.

3. **Write down how you feel and how you have been personally impacted by your unresolved feelings that are prohibiting you from dealing with your past mistakes.** It is important to embrace honesty when writing. Although others may have forgiven you or you have made heartfelt personal amends for your past transgressions, are you still unable to believe that you are worthy? God understands your feelings and He can see into your heart and soul. On the paper, write down what you are feeling, while letting your emotions flow! Guilt, despair, shame, regret, hopelessness, sadness, powerlessness, negativity, may be just a few of your feelings that you have been experiencing. Self-hatred and shame occur when we feel we have done something wrong and have not resolved the issue either externally, such as saying sorry to someone you have treated poorly, or internally, such as failing to come to terms with feelings of shame and guilt. If you do not resolve the internal struggle, the emotional pain will continue and you will

not be able to move past the self-destructive cycle of negativity and despair.

4. **Make the choice to forgive yourself.** As a conscious decision of the 'will' and one of the most beautiful gifts from God, you must choose Forgiveness. God has the power to forgive our mistakes and He wants us to embrace our own internal light so that we can learn to forgive ourselves - but it cannot begin until you make the decision to forgive. The freedom of choice is one of God's greatest blessings that He has bestowed upon us and it is part of His heavenly plan. Forgiveness is a living powerful energy, just like love. Think about and imagine yourself being overwhelmed with the energy of forgiveness. Imagine the feeling of being swept up in the enchantment of forgiveness. Be kind and gentle to yourself. Let go and trust God. Lean on God. Allow yourself to feel your own love, God's love, and make the conscious choice to forgive yourself.

5. **Acknowledge your forgiveness to God.** Take your transgression list to God and acknowledge your forgiveness to Him. Ask God to heal your emotional wounds and help you move forward without regret and let go of the past."Lord, I come to You today and release my guilt and shame. I forgive myself for _____. At this moment, I choose not to hold these offenses against

myself, but put them into Your Hands. I release my past sins of _____ into Your Hands." Now believe God has forgiven you and sit a moment to bask in His grace and mercy.

6. **Pray and ask forgiveness for people you have hurt.** Allow your painful emotions to be released so you can give them to the Lord. Find a private and meaningful way to get rid of the list forever. This physical exercise can be very emotionally and spiritually liberating. Whether you decide to burn the list, shred it, tear it into pieces and throw it into a wastebasket, or tear it into pieces and scatter it into a river or ocean, visualize your past mistakes being torn up into tiny pieces and drifting away in a magical abyss. Create a new plan to experience more, learn more, strengthen your spirituality, and to develop and grow as a person.

Fully accepting yourself and that you are unconditionally entitled to forgiveness is essential to moving forward. Becoming 'born again' includes the act of forgiving yourself. The Lord does not want us to dwell on past mistakes. God wants us to learn from our past transgressions and grow spiritually - our lives as Christians encompasses who we are in the present and what we will become in the future, walking in God's forgiveness and love. So give yourself a miraculous free gift that is priceless– The Gift of Self-Forgiveness!

Prayer:

Heavenly Father,

Every moment with You is precious.

Alone with You in this moment of meditation and prayer, I release any unresolved feelings of forgiveness in my life.

Help me through this healing process of forgiveness.

I release to You any unresolved feelings that I have toward myself. I understand that not forgiving myself is disobedience toward You.

Forgive me for any pain that I have caused in the lives of others. Forgive me for not letting go of the past and moving forward in love.

I experience now the relief of forgiveness to the depths of my being.

Heavenly Father, I acknowledge and give thanks for Your love that strengthens me, comforts and soothes me emotionally, mentally, physically and spiritually.

In the complete fullness of Your Love, I can and do forgive myself.

Thank you, Heavenly Father, for healing my heart and bringing Joy and Meaning back into my life.

In the Name of Jesus, Amen.

How to Forgive Yourself

It is not easy to forgive yourself. It takes the grace and love of God. When you spend time in His powerful presence, you will learn to love and trust Him. In time, you will be able to forgive yourself because you have asked for His forgiveness and you believe He has forgiven you. In the fullness of God's love, we forgive ourselves. Wherever we are, God is there with us, and all is well. Thank You God, for your healing, guidance, and love.

Who Do You Need to Forgive

One of the greatest gifts God gives to us is forgiveness. The reason it's such a magnificent gift is because it is such a wonderful and all-encompassing one- it covers all of our flaws and faults. When God forgives us, He does it whole-heartedly with no reservations or conditions, allowing us to heal from all of our hurts and sorrows. We don't have to earn his forgiveness or deserve it in some way - it simply washes over us from His full and loving heart !

God, Please Heal My Hurt and Unforgiveness.

God's forgiveness washes away the hurt in our lives and helps us to heal from the bitterness and pain that may be lodged in our own hearts. The hard part is passing that forgiveness on to other people - forgiveness is not easy for us, because we look around at those we need to forgive and we see that they have flaws or have made mistakes and we want to hold on to those past hurts and grievances. But that's where we're making a mistake - because *true* forgiveness, the forgiveness of God that truly comes from the heart, is a gift freely given to those who don't deserve it!

When next you feel God's forgiveness washing over you, remember to take that next step and release those people in your life that have caused you pain or sorrow. Allow your heart to forgive them and give them one of the greatest gifts there is to heal the human spirit.

> *"And forgive us our debts, as we forgive our debtors."*
> *—Matthew 6:12*

It's easy to ask God to do things for us, but we can't forget that God also requires something of us - He wants us to treat others like we would want to be treated. How can we get down on our knees and ask Him to forgive us for all of our many sins and transgressions when we are so unwilling to let go of the petty mistakes and hurts that others have inflicted on us?

> *"Whenever you stand praying, forgive, if you have anything against anyone; so that your Father in heaven may also forgive you."*
> *—Mark 11:25*

Forgiveness is the first step toward healing hurt and pain. God's love helps us to forgive. His forgiveness gives us the strength to turn toward others and express our own forgiveness, opening the way to a brighter future without rancor or grudges. We may not always have the opportunity to forgive someone in person, yet we can forgive then in our heart and mind, blessing them in our prayers.

It may be even more difficult to forgive ourselves than it is to forgive others. We often remember words we would like to take back or actions we regret years later. Through forgiving ourselves, we release the negativity and wasted energy we carry around and allow more positive, loving thoughts to fill our mind and heart. We must remember that God knows what is best for us, and isn't it presumptuous for us to think that He has forgiven us, but that we might know better than Him? After all, if we won't forgive ourselves, we are insinuating that we aren't deserving of forgiveness, despite God's opinion that we ARE ! So let go of your self-hatred, pain and unforgiveness - you ARE worthy of self-forgiveness, God has already assured you of that !

No one and nothing can compete with God's love. There is no way to alter the past. When you look back in unforgiveness, you are cutting yourself off from the opportunities God is offering you for a real future based on His love and forgiveness. Let God forgive you and heal you - and allow yourself to forgive yourself and others who may have hurt you. Know that the pain and hurt will pass and God's promise for your life will be delivered. God has something special in mind for you !

Our relationships are blessed through the transforming power of God's love. With the forgiveness we express today, we open the way to a brighter future.

Through this loving act, we free ourselves and others from the past, and we open the way to a brighter future.

When Your Diagnosis is Cancer- God Will Never Leave You

A diagnosis of cancer is a terrible thing. When we hear those dreaded words, "I'm sorry, but it is cancer," most of us immediately go into full panic mode. We wonder what we will do, we wonder how long we have to live, we wonder who will care for our children while we are sick, we wonder how much pain we will be in...and the list goes on! We "wonder," but what we are really doing is *worrying*.

Any doctor will tell you that worrying won't help and the stress of worrying too much can actually make matters worse. But even strong Christians begin to worry when facing a diagnosis like cancer. We wonder where God has gone, or why He afflicted us with cancer. The problem is, we aren't asking the right questions and we are letting our fears overcome our faith when we ask such questions!

God doesn't give us cancer. Repeat that thought to yourself, "God didn't give me cancer." It's a truth that some of us forget. Keep in mind that God created for us a loving and beautiful world that was filled with plenty and void of pain and suffering. That world changed when man sinned and fell from God's

Grace. So we live in a world with the pain of loss and the pain of suffering. It is simply a part of living in an imperfect world!

Don't personalize your cancer; don't look for someone to blame. Cancer is an impersonal, random disease that has nothing to do with God and everything to do with living in a sinful, fallen world. It is simply a result of being alive in a human, imperfect world. We can't pin our misfortunes on God, because God is always working to give us great blessings in life, *despite* the fallen nature of our world.

So where is God when the diagnosis is cancer? He's right where He has always been – right by your side, ready to help you through the pain and suffering, ready to bestow His healing touch and blessings. If you want to find God, just ask Him! Once you acknowledge God and ask for His help, you will find Him. He is just waiting for you to reach out for Him!

God's presence in the face of cancer is miraculous! He is able to be a firm and loving presence in the face of the most frightening disease in the world, and His strength and power is so overwhelming that He can grant you peace and give you comfort despite the suffering you are going through. All you need to do is have Faith – and if you have faith, you can overcome it's great enemy, fear.

So as you come to terms with the diagnosis of cancer, remember that God is right here, waiting for you to call on Him.

Don't let fear overcome you, but pray instead for God's healing touch and the comfort of His loving arms. He will cradle you in His love and give you all that you need to triumph over cancer. All you have to do is ask!

Prayer

Dear Heavenly Father,

You are my help in every need. I know that nothing is too difficult for you. Lord, I am praying for and believing in your complete healing and restoration. Help those who are caring for me; guide their hearts and hands as they tend to my body, even as you tend to my Spirit. Grant me the peace and strength I need to cope in the days ahead.

Heavenly Father, I look to you for all guidance. Continue to grant me wisdom so that I may continue to seek you above all things.

I proclaim my complete trust in you for comfort, healing, health, strength and protection.

Thank you for all that you are in my life and all that you will be in my life. Knowing and experiencing oneness with you, I experience true healing.

Thank you, Lord, for your Word and Your healing power.

In Jesus' name,
Amen.

Healing Scriptures

"I will not die but live, and will proclaim what the Lord has done"

—Psalm 118:17

"So do not fear, for I am with you; do not be dismayed, for I am your God. I will strengthen you and help you; I will uphold you with my righteous right hand"

—Isaiah 41:10

"Let us hold unswervingly to the hope we profess, for he who promised is faithful."

—Hebrews 10:23

When Someone You Love Has Cancer

A diagnosis of cancer is devastating to anyone and can be completely overwhelming to family and friends as well as the person who has received the diagnosis. When someone you love has cancer, your feelings will probably be a mix of anger, disbelief, sorrow and fear. How can you cope with your own complex feelings and still have the strength to help your loved one?

Some people will tell you that God never gives us more than we can handle, but when you're facing the prospect of coping with cancer this probably sounds like a hollow platitude. The truth is, most people are misinterpreting what this phrase means. It doesn't mean that God has given you cancer because He knows you are strong – that wouldn't be a loving God, would it? Cancer happens to both good and bad people and isn't what God wishes for us at all. When someone tells you that "God never gives us more than we can handle," take it in stride – the true meaning is this: *God doesn't let us face sorrow without giving us everything we need to survive it!* How wonderful to know that no matter what the illness, we can cope and even triumph because God will always be there, ready to give us the strength we need to handle it.

When you are a caregiver or friend to someone with cancer, you are giving both physical and spiritual support. Turn to God and ask Him to give you the strength and peace you will need to step up and be a good friend. It can be difficult; you may ask God why this has happened to your loved one. You may even be angry with God at times. The beauty of our relationship with our Lord is that even when we are angry and lashing out at Him, He will still sustain us when we ask Him for help. It's okay to pray, "God, I'm so angry right now and I don't understand why my friend has cancer, but I still need you to help me through this."

What Your Friend with Cancer Needs

Someone with cancer needs to be accepted and loved just as they are. Don't try to "fix" them, don't nag them to see more doctors, and don't tell them that everything will "be okay." Watch your words, because each one is important to a cancer patient. The words, "I will help you through this," will be music to their ears. You are promising to be there for them, which is a promise you can keep. Empty promises of a miracle cure or miraculous recovery aren't appreciated because the patient knows you can't honestly make those promises. Don't cover up your own sorrow or discomfort with empty promises.

Be specific and direct when talking with your loved one, telling them what you can do for them and reassuring them that you will be there for them.

Avoid giving advice to a loved one with cancer. They may ask your opinion on occasion, but as time goes by they will decide for themselves how they want to proceed. Remember, they are feeling like their lives are out of control, so giving unwanted advice will only make them feel more confused and out of control. Constantly trying to talk them into more doctors or a different approach will only reinforce their feelings of being out of control of their lives. It's okay to ask if they've had a second opinion, but don't keep pushing them to follow a different path than the one they've chosen. They have probably already agonized over their decision, prayed about it and are ready to move on.

Don't make it all about the cancer. When you spend time with a loved one who has cancer, be sure you focus on other parts of his or her life so that they can feel relatively normal sometimes. Look for ways to share and grow in your relationship that have nothing to do with their illness. If they aren't feeling strong enough to work or take part in their usual activities, find ways to keep them involved in life. Learn a new hobby or craft together, organize family photo albums, exchange childhood stories or design and research your family tree. They will cherish the opportunity to step outside of their cancer and focus on enjoying the moments you create with them.

Share your life with your loved one. They don't want to talk about themselves and their cancer all the time, and if you stop sharing your own life with them, they will feel like they already have one foot in the grave and that you are already pulling away from them. Don't worry that your own problems may seem "trivial" to a cancer patient. They will welcome hearing about your own problems occasionally and will be happy to know that you still value their opinion. You will be giving them a great gift if you let them know they are still vibrant individuals who can contribute to your life. Ask how they would handle a child discipline problem, ask for new recipe suggestions, ask for help picking out a birthday gift for a friend – the important thing is to *ask!*

Listen, listen, listen! Cancer patients don't want to hear your solutions when they complain about the chemo, confess their anger with God, or tell you they are afraid of dying. They want to be heard. They want to be able to express themselves in a safe, non-judgmental way and know that they won't be criticized or corrected. Sometimes just letting go of their emotions and shouting it out, talking it out or crying it all can bring enormous relief. So listen and then hold their hand, wrap them in your arms or whatever feels right to let them know you aren't shocked or upset by their feelings. Being completely and lovingly accepted despite their doubts or fears will give your loved ones a tremendous sense of peace.

Remember that You are God's gift to your loved one! When someone you love is diagnosed with cancer, you may think, "How can God let this happen?" But cancer is an illness of his world, not God's design; it strikes *despite* God's love for us. The right perspective is essential here – take a moment to think about God's mercy and loving kindness in sending your loved one a wonderful caregiver, supporter and friend in *YOU*. How wonderful that God has provided a strong, loving friend for your loved one, and how blessed you are that you can make the ordeal of cancer more bearable for them! God is at work in all things, and He has given you a great opportunity to be His own angel on earth for someone with cancer.

Let God Help You be a Strong and True Blessing to Your Loved One with Cancer

But what about when you become overwhelmed yourself when someone you love has cancer? How can you cope without letting them down? First, remember that you don't have to be everything to your loved one. You don't have to always be talking, doing or physically caring for them. Often, the simple fact of your physical presence will be enough to reassure them that they are not alone. You don't have to always be "on." You can simply watch television, read a book or meditate while you keep a cancer patient company. A person by their side can go a long way in keeping them from feeling isolated or alone.

Next, forget about being the perfect caregiver. Everything you do can help, but that *doesn't* mean you have to do everything! Learn to let go of what isn't important. So what if the dusting doesn't get done or there are toys scattered around the room? So what if your kids are eating quick meals from the take-out place occasionally? In the face of cancer, don't dwell on being perfect, but on being *present in the moment.* The little details will work themselves out.

Be forgiving. Forgive yourself for your mistakes, uncertainty and anger or sorrow. Forgive others who may not be able to cope as well as you do. Forgive your loved one for putting you through all of this fear and sorrow. Turn to God and admit your own fears, then ask Him to forgive you for being all too human in the face of cancer. Soon, you'll realize that despite the tremendous sorrow and uncertainty of your loved one's cancer diagnosis, you are moving forward in a new and closer relationship with them and with God. By turning to Him and forgiving yourself and others, you open yourself to the rich joy that can be found even in times of trial.

Finally, don't be afraid to ask God to heal your loved one! Not every prayer is answered in the way we hope, but every prayer is heard. He may bring your loved one release from pain, the strength to cope with it, remission or a hundred other results. He knows what is right and good for your loved one even when they are suffering from cancer, and He will hear and listen to your prayers. Loving prayers are one of the most valuable gifts you can give a loved one with cancer!

Prayer

Dear Heavenly Father,

You are my help in every need. I know that nothing is too hard for you. Heavenly Father, I am praying and hoping now for the complete healing and restoration of (fill-in-the-blank with the name of your loved one). Guide my heart and hands so that I may be a true comfort as their caregiver. Give me the peace and strength I need to cope in the days ahead.

Heavenly Father I look to you for guidance. Continue to grant me wisdom. Wisdom to seek you above all things.

I proclaim my complete trust in you for healing, health, strength, wisdom and protection.

Thank you for all that you are in my life and all that you will be in my life. Give me the strength to share your loving kindness with my loved one so that they may experience joy and closeness to You in the face of their diagnosis.

Knowing my oneness with you, Heavenly Father, I pray that (fill-in-the blank with your loved one's name) experience true healing.

Thank you, Lord, for sending your word and your healing power and your support during these painful times.

In the powerful Name of Jesus,

Amen

Scriptures to meditate on as a caregiver:

"I look up to the mountains—
 does my help come from there?
My help comes from the Lord,
 who made heaven and earth!"

—Psalm 121:1-2

Wait patiently for the Lord.
 Be brave and courageous.
 Yes, wait patiently for the Lord.

—Psalm 27:14

How to Pray Effectively - Seven Steps to Answered Prayers

There is power in prayer; it has no boundaries or borders, but many of us aren't sure how to get started or what to say. Prayer is simply having a conversation with God. This sounds intimidating, but it doesn't have to be. Having the right ingredients or elements in your prayers are much more important than whether they sound fancy or elegant. In fact, you can talk to God just like you would talk to a parent or best friend. So forget about *how* you say it, and focus on what you want and need to say.

The Bible talks about "petitioning" God in prayer – this means to earnestly plea or implore. To "present your requests" to God is simply to tell Him specifically what you need. Praying about each worry or need in your life shuts out worry because it invites God to be involved in every area of your life, and when He is engaged in each aspect of your life, there is nothing to fear.

Here are seven steps that can help you pray more effectively and deepen your relationship with the Lord:

1. **Acknowledge your personal relationship with God as His child.** Recognize that God is holy and powerful and give Him the reverence that He deserves. Having a loving relationship with God is like that between a parent and child.

2. **Acknowledge your respect for who God is.** Commit your life to God each day, promising to live according to His will. Praise God during prayer and throughout your day, becoming absorbed in Him.

   "If you abide in me, and my words abide in you, you will ask what you desire, and it shall be done for you."

   –John 15:7

3. **Confess your sins.** It is so important to ask God to forgive your sins and ask Him to continue to love and care for you. Repentance is a sign of your understanding that you have – like all of us have – broken God's commands, and are sorry for what you have done. By acknowledging that our sins have separated us temporarily from God, we are once again brought closer to Him.

4. **Ask God in prayer.** Many of us feel guilty if we ask God for anything, fearing that we aren't worthy and that we are being demanding, or that we might anger God. It is just the opposite – by asking God, we are acknowledging that

we can't do it alone; we are recognizing our need for His divine intervention and showing that we trust in Him to help us. Nothing could make God happier!

5. **Be Specific.** Prayers can be quite general, asking for blessings from the Lord, but it is okay to be specific, too. When we ask the Lord to help us find a better job, resolve a problem with our spouse or anything else that is personal to us, we are opening our innermost hearts to Him. This personal, private kind of prayer asking for specific help tells God that we have faith in Him to watch over us in small ways as well as big ones. He wants to be the Lord of our lives in all things large and small, so it is fine to pray to find a way to get a new dryer if yours breaks down!

6. **Have an attitude of Expectancy and Faith.** Trust that God can answer any prayer. Have faith that God will hear you when you pray according to His will. Do not pray in fear or out of desperation because "nothing else has worked." Pray confidently, with the faith that God will fulfill your expectations in the best way possible for you, born out of His divine wisdom.

"Listen to me! You can pray for anything, and if you believe, you will have it."

-Mark 11:24

7. **Pray in Jesus' name.** When we pray in Jesus' name, we enter into a relationship with Jesus Christ, God's own son. We are able to take full advantage of Jesus' death on the cross as a payment for our sins by acknowledging His sacrifice in our prayers. It also ties us to the new life of Christ's resurrection. The secret of our Christian life is also the secret of praying – doing all in Jesus' name.

"Whatever you ask in my name, that I will do."
—John 14:13

Every prayer is important. Every prayer counts. Our prayers exalts Him for who He is. There is power in prayer. In His presence is where we will find our greatest blessings.

God Will Diminish Our Sight to Increase Our Faith

Ever feel like you're staggering around in the dark? Not sure of where you're going, or maybe even where you've been? You are not alone. God is present. But faith is not always easy, is it? Faith requires courage, and perseverance. The book of Hebrews tells us, "Now faith is being sure of what we hope for and certain of what we do not see." (11:1) How is it possible to be certain of what we cannot see? Therein lies the mystery of faith. Even though the Bible tells us in Corinthians 5:7 that "We live by faith, not by sight," the Bible never claims it will be easy. Faith is a great teacher and a great teacher doesn't make it easy for the students. Faith often gives us the test *before* we receive the lesson.

We are engineered to search for purpose in life, and when we don't find it, when we don't understand why things are the way they are, it can be disheartening, maybe even devastating. These are the moments when God calls us to be reduced to faith, for then it is when we are leaning wholly on our faith in God that we are most strong. (2 Corinthians 12:10)

There is a purpose to it all. Romans 8:28 tells us: "And we know that in all things God works for the good of those who love him, who have been called according to his purpose." It is no accident that there is only one you. It is no accident that out of the billions of people on earth, out of all the possible DNA codes, there is only one you. God designed you to seek Him and to need Him. Your faith honors and pleases God in a unique and precious way.

If we knew it all now, if we had all the answers now, we would have no need for God. God doesn't want to just give us wisdom. God wants us to develop a personal relationship with Him, a relationship of dependence. He wants us to trust in Him fully, to find rest in His arms. Only then can we know the meaning of peace, because peace comes from faith.

The Bible tells us in Philippians 4:7 that "the peace of God, which transcends all understanding, will guard your hearts and your minds in Christ Jesus." The peace transcends understanding. It rises above, it goes beyond, it is more powerful than simple understanding. We are not meant to understand, not yet, and if we take a step back and think on this, we might see the beauty in it. God makes life a mystery so that we will need Christ, so that our hearts will desire Him, and will know the peace and awesome joy that comes from that desire. It's like falling in love.

How do we receive this peace? Through prayer, and through reading God's Word. In the book of Mark, a follower of Jesus exclaims, "I do believe; help me overcome my unbelief!" When you don't understand, when you are suffering from 'unbelief,' when you're feeling lost, take it to God in prayer. Take all your concerns, all your worries, all your fears to God. He will hear you. He will also lead you. He will use the trials of life to shape you for His purpose.

> *"I will instruct you and teach you in the way you should go; I will counsel you and watch over you."*
> *-Psalm 32:8*

There will be times when life's circumstances are so painful, we beg to know *why*. How could God let such a thing happen? Death of a loved one. Social injustice. Divorce. Poverty. Hunger. Cancer. Though we do not yet understand the purpose of such trials, by leaning on God, by trusting that one day, we will understand, we are driven to seek the relationship with our Creator that we were designed to find, and that relationship will allow us to experience divine love. And that love just might be more powerful, more important, than understanding.

> *"Trust in the Lord with all your heart and lean not on your own understanding."*
> *—Proverbs 3:5*

Whatever we need, whatever we think we need, God is the answer. With complete faith and trust in God, we not only survive- we thrive !

Walk by Faith and Leave the Results to God

Walking by faith is easy when we get the results we are looking for, isn't it? When our prayers are answered the way we want them to be and everything happens the way we want, it's easy to have faith.

But the real test of Christian faith is in facing the silence of being "on hold" with God. Faith is a hard teacher. Faith gives us the test before we get the lesson. Sometimes we pray and pray to God and it seems like He might not be listening because we don't get an answer right away. But we aren't looking at it properly when we think that way. The truth is, sometimes God's answer to our prayer is, "No," or "Not right now."

Because God is seeing the situations of our lives so much more clearly than we could ever hope to, He can make the right decisions for us, even if we can't see that clearly sometimes. Remember, too, that faith means we believe in Him and His time table - we have to trust that He knows what is right for us and when it is right - and we must not ask Him to prove it ! That's not faith - that's doubt.

> *"Now faith is the assurance of things hoped for, the conviction of things not seen."*
>
> *–Hebrews 11:1*

There's a country song by popular singer Garth Brooks that was very popular a few years ago that has line in that says, "Sometimes I thank God for unanswered prayers, so remember when you're talking to the Man upstairs, just because he doesn't answer, it doesn't mean He don't care…" In the song, the singer sees his old high school sweetheart and recalls that he prayed every night that God would let him marry this girl. Now he looks at his wife and thanks God that He didn't answer those old prayers - because the Lord knew that the right woman was waiting for him.

Do you have that kind of faith in the Lord? Can you pray and not be disappointed that sometimes what you are praying for isn't what you get? It's hard, isn't it? But the Lord knows that it isn't good for Him to answer everybody's prayer to win the lottery, or even every prayer to get a particular job. Why? Because it's easy for us to forget that we only see things in the here and now - but God sees a plan for us that stretches far into the future and He's planning for the rest of our life and into eternity.

Continue to pray, but do so in faith, knowing that God is with you in every moment. Whether you are seeking employment, healing, new friendships, a renewal of love or a change in your own heart, give it time. Don't give in to impatience or demand that God do it "now". Trust in God to work in and through every circumstance you face and teach you something in every experience. Leaving the results - and the timing - to God will enrich your life in ways you can't foresee but that He has prepared for you out of His great and abiding love for you.

Remember the Powerful Benefits of Christian Faith:

- Faith is the assurance that there will be answer to all we take to God in prayers.

- Faith is holding to the blessings we know to be true, even when the world and our lives indicate otherwise.

- Faith proclaims that nothing is impossible for us if we rely on the power of God to guide us through every situation.

- Faith in God uplifts us and gives us the courage to move forward.

- Faith in God will sustain us and bring us successfully through every crisis.

- Faith in God means you do not doubt yourself.

> *"Have faith in God. Truly I tell you if you say to this mountain, 'Be taken up and thrown into the sea,' and if you do not doubt in your heart, but believe that what you say will come to pass, it will be done for you."*
>
> *—Mark 11:22-23*

So the next time you pray, praise God, ask for His guidance and be willing to ask for what you need. But remember that true faith requires that asking also meaning resting in the assurance that God will see to the results without your help. Walk in faith and leave the results to God - He can handle it ! Honor Him by your Faith.

How to Discover Your Life's Purpose

Your life's purpose isn't always easy to understand. Many of us go through our lives without ever knowing what our true purpose is; we go through the motions of holding down a job and supporting our families without really knowing what our *purpose* or our *true calling* is. Why is that?

Our purpose in life has to be based on factors that will always be relevant, and the only thing you have that you will always have is your spirituality. As spiritual beings we all have a purpose, and when that purpose begins to dawn on you, you will carry it into your chosen fields of expression.

> *"The Lord will fulfill his purpose for me: your love, O Lord, endures forever - do not abandon the works of your hands."*
>
> *–Psalm 138:8*

Working at your job and taking care of your family is certainly a part of God's plan for your life – your family is very important – but it may not be the only thing that He has in mind for you. So how do you discover the fullness of God's plan for you? How do you know when you are fulfilling the true purpose of your life?

We have to discover if our lives are pleasing in the eyes of God. We must look for the signs, both small and large, that what we are doing is what God wants for us and is spiritually right for us. Sometimes this is easy. Moses received some very clear signs that his purpose was to lead his people out of captivity in Egypt – the Lord spoke to him from a burning bush and performed miraculous miracles like turning a wooden staff into a snake before his eyes. Most of us don't get such unmistakable messages that say, "You need to follow this path."

But if we pray each night and ask God to give us a sign that we have chosen the right path in our careers or who our friends are or what choices we are making for our families, we will be heard. Sometimes the answer isn't the one we really want. Perhaps we begin to feel that little bit of doubt that we haven't chosen the best group of friends or that we aren't doing what we should be to help our neighbors…whatever little nudges we feel in our conscience are really God's way of gently reminding us that we may be straying from our purpose. Sometimes God doesn't shout from a burning bush – sometimes He quietly guides us back onto the path toward our purpose. The result is the same – we will get there at the right time – in God's time!

The most important thing we have to do is accept the Lord's guidance and use our talents properly to fulfill our purpose once we know what that purpose is. In Jesus' Parable of the Talents, a slave owner gave three slaves some coins called 'talents' to keep for him while he traveled. Two of them invested the coins and turned them into more money, while the third simply hid the money until the master returned.

We must be like the servants who invested the talents – whatever our purpose is, we must fully invest our own unique talents so that we fulfill our purpose to the best of our ability and increase their value so that our purpose doesn't languish.

The next time you ask yourself "What is my purpose in life?" don't turn to a career counselor, friends or co-workers. Turn to the one constant, sure thing in your life – your Spiritual Guide. Get down on your knees and ask the Lord about your Purpose and open yourself up to all the possibilities. It may be something as simple as being the best possible example of a Godly woman that you can be at your current job and in your family, or it may be to walk an entirely different path.

The key is to open your heart and your soul to God's signs wherever they are found – in the still, silent moments when you question what you are doing, in the 'coincidences' that seem to be leading you in a particular direction, and in those moments of joy when you realize that you've taken a step in the right direction.

God is waiting to help you discover your purpose – just ask Him!

The Powerful Benefits of Tithing

No one likes to think about tithing when it comes to God and His church. If most of us were honest, we would admit that it is far easier to pray, sing God's praises and help others than it is to turn over 10% of everything we earn to the Lord. Yet God blesses those who tithe, and it is one of the most basic Biblical tests of our faithfulness and stewardship. In fact, the word "tithe" actually means "tenth."

We are so often thinking about all of our own needs that we put tithing last on our list and tell ourselves, "If I had anything left over, I would certainly give my ten percent, but I never have anything left." But if you tithed *first* by setting aside your ten percent for God before paying the bills, you would be surprised to find that you *can* give your ten percent. You would simply have less for things you don't really need. And here's the best part – God will reward you for your faithfulness!

God wants to bless us, but it is difficult to trust us with riches on earth when we won't share our blessings. In Luke 16:11, Jesus said,

> "...if you have not been faithful in handling worldly wealth, who will trust you with true riches?"

As a church, we are trying to further God's kingdom here on earth and bring the comfort of the Lord to other's lives. Have we saved the world? No. Have we comforted everyone? No. Have we abolished need? No. The Lord asks that we "put our money where our mouths are." To give back 10% of what we have to try and reach that place where no one is in need.

And yet, God is a loving God. He has not asked us for *everything* we have. He knows we have to feed our own children and put a roof over our heads. He even knows we have to pay the IRS! He said, "Render unto Caesar that which is Caesar's." The IRS is today's equivalent of Caesar! God hasn't ignored the realities of living in today's world. He doesn't ask for all of it, or even most of it. Not even one quarter of it! Just one tenth. But it still sounds like a lot, doesn't it? So how do we give up one tenth of what we earn and not ruin ourselves financially?

Well, we turn over so much to God – our cares, our concerns, our personal problems and our health issues. We say, "Dear Lord, heal my friend." But God is not a doctor. We say, "Jesus, help my spouse and I to get our marriage back on track." But God isn't Doctor Phil. But how many of us have said, "God, guide me in my financial decisions. Help me live and work in order to return to you as much as I can for your work here on earth?"

We pray for health, we pray for guidance, we pray for comfort. Why *not* turn our financial concerns – and our money – over to God? Why *not* give back a mere slice of what God gives us back to Him? And it is all His, isn't it?

Part of the problem is giving up control. When we tithe, we don't know how the money will be used, so we hesitate to hand over our money. But when there is a fundraiser for something specific – a new bell tower at the church, to help a family we know, or for a particular charity – we always find a way to give. Why wait? Aren't there *always* people in need? Ministries to be served? Missionaries without funding?

If each and every one of us tithed freely to God, no fundraisers would be needed! There would be plenty to go around! As Americans, we don't realize how truly God has blessed us financially. We say, "Lord, it is hard to tithe." But it shouldn't be, particularly when we have been blessed by God. *Because with our success comes the responsibility to use it wisely to help others and further God's kingdom.*

It is easy to forget that our success comes from God's grace. He has blessed us with so many things – shouldn't we thank Him by using our blessings in ways that would gladden His heart?

Tithing ensures that our needs will be met and gives back to God what was always His. God is honored when we are faithful. When we acknowledge that God is the true owner and giver of all that we have, we will be rewarded in countless ways.

Ken Blanchard, the author of *The One Minute Manager,* said, "I absolutely believe in the Power of Tithing and giving back. My own experience about all the blessings I've had in my life is that the more I give away, the more comes back. That is the way life works, and that is the way energy works."

> *"…they gave as much as they were able, and even beyond their ability. Entirely on their own, they urgently pleaded with us for the privilege of sharing in this service to the saints. And they did not do as we expected, but they gave themselves first to the Lord and then to us in keeping with God's will… just as you excel in everything—in faith, in speech, in knowledge, in complete earnestness and in your love for us - see that you also excel in this grace of giving."*
> *–2 Corinthians 8:1-8*

So the next time you think about giving to God, remember that all of your blessings came from Him, and give back your ten percent with a happy heart. He gives us so much and asks for so little!

When Life Hurts - God Can Heal Your Emotional Wounds

God is love. It's in the Bible. We've all heard this part. It's been said so many times, it's almost lost its meaning. God is love? In a world like this? Well, so what! But if we meditate on the idea, it returns to its profound roots. God is love. The Book of First John tells us that "love comes from God," that "everyone who loves has been born of God and knows God." Isn't that a great feeling? We know God because we know love?

So what does this have to do with my emotional wounds? With all of the painful things that have happened to me? Well, love is the only cure. And God is that love.

According to Scripture, God has a soft spot for those who suffer. Psalm 34:18 reads, "The Lord is close to the brokenhearted, and saves those who are crushed in spirit." Psalm 147:3 reads, "He heals the brokenhearted and binds up their wounds." According to Scripture, God knows how many hairs are on your head (Matthew 10:30). He knows the condition of your heart (Psalm 139). And He cares about every second of your pain (1 Peter 5:7, John 3:16).

God is an all-sufficient love, and a relationship with Him can and will heal your emotional wounds. Consider the story of

Luke 8: Jesus was walking along and the crowds were pushing in on Him and almost crushing Him. All of a sudden He turned around and said, "Who touched me?" The disciples, a bit baffled, were like, well Lord, several hundred people are touching you, and Jesus said, "Someone touched me; I know that power has gone out of me." The woman who had grabbed at His cloak came forward and told Jesus how she had touched Him for healing and that she had already been healed. Jesus said to her, "Daughter, your faith has healed you. Go in peace."

Faith can heal us too. We just have to believe and we have to reach out for Jesus. In John 16:23, Christ says, "I tell you the truth, my Father will give you whatever you ask in my name." In Philippians Chapter 4, Paul tells us to take everything to God in prayer, "Do not be anxious about anything, but in everything, by prayer and petition, with thanksgiving, present your requests to God. And the peace of God, which transcends all understanding, will guard your hearts and your minds in Christ Jesus." What a promise is this! We just have to pray about our hurt, we just have to take our broken hearts to God, and He will replace our pain with peace. If the whole world knew this, wouldn't we be spending most of our time on our knees? It is a peace that transcends our understanding. That is a peace that sounds even stronger than my pain.

God wants you to use your emotional wounds to grow closer to Him. In 2 Corinthians, Chapter 12, Christ says, "My grace is sufficient for you, for my power is made perfect in weakness." Paul goes on to write, "For when I am weak, then I am strong." This is a paradox for many of us, because we all want to be strong. And we can be, in Christ. In God, we can be stronger than we can ever be alone. If our emotional suffering brings us closer to God, and as a result, makes us stronger, maybe our wounds are also blessings.

Christ gave a sermon on a mountain and it was such an important event that it is described in both Matthew and Luke. In this sermon, Jesus stood tradition on its head. He did so by blessing people who were then considered unlikely recipients. He said, "Blessed are the poor in spirit, for theirs is the kingdom of heaven. Blessed are those who mourn, for they will be comforted. Blessed are the meek, for they will inherit the earth. Blessed are the pure in heart, for they will see God." Are you poor in spirit? Are you mourning? Have you suffered for your meekness? The good news is, if you seek God, you will be blessed. In this famous Sermon on the Mount, Jesus was describing God's children. God wants you to be His child. He wants you to need Him, and when you allow yourself to need Him, that's when the healing begins.

> *"And hope does not disappoint us, because God has poured out his love into our hearts by the Holy Spirit, whom he has given us."*
>
> —*Romans 5:5*

Choose to Be Free from Your Past

I don't know many people who live entirely without regrets. Unless we've been blessed with a significant bump on the head, most of us carry around memories we'd rather forget. But it is up to us to decide whether we strain our muscles dragging this baggage around or whether we unpack our issues and deal with them. (We can always repack, right?)

In Chapter 8 of the Book of John, Jesus was teaching in the temple courts, and some teachers brought in a woman who had been caught cheating on her husband. They made her stand in front of everyone and they said to Jesus, "Teacher, this woman was caught in the act of adultery. In the Law, Moses commanded us to stone such women. Now what do you say?"

Have you ever felt like this woman? Have you ever felt condemned for something? It might not have been adultery. However, we all have felt condemned for something. I know I have. Not that anyone has ever attempted to stone me, thank God, but I've had metaphorical rocks hurled at me plenty of times. Do you know what Jesus said to her accusers? He said, "If any one of you is without sin, let him be the first to throw a stone at her." The teachers wandered off and the woman stood where she was, until Jesus stood up and said to her, "Woman, where are they? Has no one condemned you?" "No one, sir," she said. "Then neither do I condemn you," Jesus declared. "Go now and leave your life of sin."

There are many lessons to be taken from this simple story. First of all, Jesus calls the teachers out: Hey, we all have a past. We all have issues. Every one of you has something you'd rather not share. Then he tells the unnamed woman, "I do not condemn you." This might not have meant as much to her then as it does to us now. We don't know whether or not she was aware that she was receiving a pardon from God Himself. But we can look at this scene and know that Christ was saying to this woman, "I am not judging you, go on now, get on with your life, and stop cheating on your husband."

Can this apply to any mistakes we've made in our pasts? Christ sacrificed Himself on the cross so that we could be forgiven our sins. If we wallow in unnecessary, harmful guilt, then we are not fully accepting His sacrifice, His selfless gift. If He wanted us to feel guilty, to spend time, and muscle power, dragging that baggage around, He wouldn't have made the ultimate sacrifice. He gave His life to buy our freedom. Our freedom from sin, our freedom from death, and our freedom from our own pasts. Later on in this same chapter, Christ says, "Then you will know the truth, and the truth will set you free." Jesus Christ is this Truth.

So, you're asking, what about those of us who have suffered due to no fault of our own? Yes, painful things certainly happen to innocent people. Victims of disease, oppression, rape, child abuse, adultery, the list goes on. Life is not fair.

Faith is easier said than done. It is difficult for those who have truly suffered to believe that their suffering can lead to a greater purpose. In the Book of Ephesians, Chapter 1, Verse 11, the Apostle Paul writes, "In him we are also chosen, having been predestined according to the plan of him who works out everything in conformity with the purpose of his will." Believers are chosen by God. Sometimes, when we are suffering, or when we have suffered, we wish we hadn't been chosen, but the truth is, it feels good to be chosen, especially when we are able and willing to believe that our suffering, our pain, is going to work out for the purpose of His will. God is love. God's will leads to love, even if there are some unlovely bumps in the road.

Writer George Bernard Shaw wrote, "If you can't get rid of the skeleton in your closet, you might as well teach it to dance." This is an apt metaphor for creativity, and that's how this quote is usually interpreted, but it also reminds me of God's Will. Oftentimes, we are able to use our past, our mistakes, or our time spent as innocent victims, to love others, to glorify God. Recovering alcoholics can minister to those struggling with alcoholism. Ex-convicts can go minister in the jails. Rape victims can counsel other rape victims.

Suffering is difficult, but we need to know that God is not judging us. Psalm 103 reads, "As far as the east is from the west, so far has he removed our transgressions from us." That's a long way! That's infinity! God has forgiven us. In light of His sacrifice, it is the least we can do to forgive ourselves. He has also asked us to use everything in our power for His glory. Is it possible to use your past to bless others? Is this the way to truly be free of it? The answer is a resounding- Yes !

No matter what has happened in your past, you are forever sustained by the love of God.

Emotional Healing
- Breaking Your Silence

Some things are difficult to discuss. Sometimes it's easier to keep things buried within us. But buried pain doesn't heal very well, now does it? Buried pain stays buried and festers, sometimes surfacing when we least expect it, often, when we are least equipped to deal with it.

It's better to help ourselves heal *before* issues come to a head. It's better to break the silence. And the easiest place to start is with a silent prayer.

We all have things we'd rather keep quiet. Some of us have been mistreated, abused, neglected. Some of us have been sexually assaulted. Some of us have been humiliated and defeated. This doesn't sound like good news, does it?

But maybe it is. The Bible tells us in Psalm 34:18 that "The Lord is close to the brokenhearted and saves those who are crushed in spirit." God is there for the people who need Him most. That's me. Could that be you too?

Does it really help to talk to God about our pain? In John 14:27, Jesus says, "Peace I leave with you; my peace I give you.

I do not give to you as the world gives. Do not let your hearts be troubled and do not be afraid." This verse suggests that talking to Jesus about our hurt might actually be the most beneficial conversation we can have! He can offer us a healing that surpasses the healing of the world. He can offer us a heart free of trouble or fear! All we have to do is ask.

This is often easier said then done. For those of us who believe that God already knows everything, it might feel silly to tell Him about our issues. But He wants to hear it from our hearts. He wants us to seek Him. It is by admitting our need for Him that we gain access to His healing power. For those of us who aren't even sure if we believe in a God, it might feel silly to talk to one. Lucky for us, we can start the conversation with that doubt. Nowhere in the Bible does it say God will hold back His healing power if we begin our prayer with, "Is there anybody out there?" If we are honestly seeking Him, even if we're not sure what it is we are doing, what it is we are saying, He is still listening. He will hear you. And just by beginning that conversation, we begin to heal.

And if we are feeling really brave, or really grateful, we can always thank Him for our pain. I know, that sounds crazy, right? In 2 Corinthians 12:9, Christ says, "My grace is sufficient for you, for my power is made perfect in weakness." And the Apostle Paul responds to this by saying, "Therefore, I will boast all the more gladly about my weaknesses so that Christ's power may rest on me."

I don't think Paul was suggesting that we run up and down the streets shouting that we were molested when we were young. We can, however, adopt an attitude that allows us to feel strengthened by our pain. If it is this pain that brings us closer to the all-healing power of an all-powerful God. If it takes a little bit of hell to feel the peace of heaven, maybe, just maybe, we can be grateful? Grateful for a sufficient grace, grateful for perfect power?

It might take a while to get there. We don't usually break the silence and immediately fall to our knees in gratitude. It is a process, and one that might be impossible to accomplish on our own. The first step however, is always breaking the silence. The first step has to be a conversation with God. It doesn't have to be scripted. It doesn't have to be rehearsed. It doesn't even have to make sense. We just need to open our hearts. We just need to break the silence. We just need to ask.

> *"Come to me, all you who are weary and burdened, and I will give you rest. Take my yoke upon you and learn from me, for I am gentle and humble in heart, and you will find rest for your souls. For my yoke is easy and my burden is light."*
> *—Matthew 11:28-30*

Are you feeling burdened today? Tired? Heavy? Sick of carrying around whatever lies buried in your heart? You don't have to suffer in silence alone. God will always be there for you. He is waiting on you to come to Him. God is easy to talk to. Open your heart . Start the conversation and begin to experience emotional healing in your life today. *God will heal what you reveal.*

Emotional Healing After Your Husband's Sexual Betrayal

So, your husband is looking at pornography. Maybe he's looking at it a lot. Maybe you've asked him to stop and he hasn't. Probably, this is one of the most difficult things your marriage has encountered. Maybe he's telling you it's no big deal. But your instincts are right: It is a big deal, and addiction to pornography has fractured thousands of marriages. Sexual addiction betrayal is very painful. But your marriage doesn't have to be part of the statistic. God has the power of emotional healing.

The first thing to know is: *his pornography addiction has nothing to do with you.* I have heard people suggest that men turn to pornography when they are not satisfied with their wives. This is simply not true. Many women -- beautiful, fit, sexy, slim women -- have done everything their husband asks of them, and their husband still turns elsewhere. What goes on in your husband's mind and heart is between him and God. In fact, there's nothing you can do about it. And that should take some of the pressure off you. *You can't fix your husband's problems.* Only God can. All you can do is love your husband the way you promised you would, and try your best to love him the way God loves him.

Also please know that when your gut tells you that pornography consumption is not okay, that might just be the Holy Spirit talking. Pornography is not okay, no matter what our culture tells you, no matter what anyone tells you, lust is a sin. In Matthew 5: 28, the Bible tells us: But I tell you that anyone who looks at a woman lustfully has already committed adultery with her in his heart. So, don't feel like you have to accept this behavior. But you also don't have to fix it.

So, what *do* you do? How do you deal, while maintaining your own integrity, while trying to heal from such an intimate betrayal? How do you ease your own hurt?

Two things: prayer and love. And then, more prayer.

The Bible tells me in 1 Thessalonians 5:17 to "pray continually." The King James Version reads, "Pray without ceasing." Philippians 4:6 says: Do not be anxious about anything, but in everything, by prayer and petition, with thanksgiving, present your requests to God. I know, easier said than done, right? How can you possibly be thankful that your husband watches pornography after you've gone to bed? It's not easy. But that's why God gave women the gift of prayer. Take it to God. Tell God you're angry. Ask Him to help you. The Lord is faithful.

And as for love, this might be the most difficult time you've ever tried to love your husband. But Jesus never said love would be easy. Jesus loved the people who nailed Him to a cross. And He asks us to do the same. But it is only through love, that you may show your husband the face of Christ. Preaching will not do it, because words have no effect on a heart that is not ready to receive them, just as seeds do not take root in soil that isn't ready. Hollering at your husband will not help. Loving him will. It will help your husband, and it will help you. Loving others heals us, because it brings us closer to Jesus.

I'm not suggesting that you embrace his sin. I'm not suggesting that you act like "a doormat" and pretend that his addiction does not hurt you.

I'm just saying that you try to love him through it. Try to forgive him, every day. It will not be easy. And now we're back to prayer.

Pray to God for help in loving your husband. Confess to God that you are angry, that you don't feel like loving, but ask Him to take over. Pray to God, "I can't do this one more day. I feel so awful. Please help me. Please help me to forgive, and to love. Please help me not to freak out. Not to feel bad about myself. Please help me love my husband the way You love him." And when you open your eyes from that prayer, you really might see your husband differently.

Your marriage is important. But so is your relationship with your Lord. If this trial brings you closer to your God, then it is a blessing after all. Be thankful for difficulties. Try to be thankful for your husband. Try to serve your Lord. Try to love. Christ never said it would be easy. He just said it would be beautiful.

And remember, your husband's activities have nothing to do with you. God has the power to heal the hurt of your sexual addiction betrayal. Your beauty is your own. Your dignity remains intact. You are a precious jewel. Just like Proverbs 31 says: a wife of noble character is worth far more than rubies. Walk the path to emotional healing and live a life of happiness and peace again.

Only God Needs to Know

Cast your burden upon the Lord and He will sustain you.

-Psalm 55:22

As we grow in God, we often feel the need to confess stuff from our past. It's almost like purging – we want to get rid of the mistakes that we've made in the past by sharing them with someone.

God makes a great listener. He *is* The Great Listener. And by sharing your burdens, your thoughts, your struggles, and your feelings with God, you can become free of them. Believers call it "laying it at the cross." You can take your issues to Jesus, and give them to Him. He took them all on for you two thousand years ago when He gave Himself to that cross. Laying your burdens at the cross will set you free.

By giving your burdens, whatever is weighing you down or holding you back, to God, you also free the people you love. When you give these things to God, you don't have to give them to anyone else. God is sufficient. God's grace is sufficient (2 Corinthians 12:9). No one else needs to know. Only God needs to know. He wants to be your best friend, your father, your confidante, and your Higher Power. When you've got God on your side, you don't really need anyone else.

Even after you've shared something painful or difficult with God, you might still feel the urge to share with someone else, e.g., a spouse, best friend, parent, or child. But doing this would pass your pain on to someone else.

The truth is that you don't need to burden your loved ones by sharing painful things from your past with them. God will, or already has, set you free from these things (Philippians 4:6-7). Your loved ones might not be in the same spiritual place that you are, and might not be ready to ask God to set them free as well. By sharing the mistakes of your past with someone other than God, you could weigh that person down. And you don't need to do this, because you've got God.

God can handle whatever you throw at Him. So you really don't need anyone else. If you have something in your past that is truly in your past, there is no need to bring it into the light for anyone other than God. Keep it between you and Him.

Sometimes, we think we're done with something, and then some circumstances will cause our past mistakes to rear their ugly heads. We'll see someone from our past, or hear a song, or see a movie that reminds us of something. If this happens to you, just give it all back to God in prayer. The Bible tells us to "pray without ceasing" (1 Thessalonians 5:17). Sometimes life reminds us of this truth in unpleasant ways. It still doesn't mean that you need to burden someone else. Just slow down and spend some time with God. He is sufficient. He promises.

Single Christian Women- 5 Things to Look for in a Partner

Being single is a lot of work. There is a lot of pressure on single women to "find a man," to get married, and to start a family. In the Christian community, this pressure can be even more intense, as traditional values often put a lot of importance on the marriage model. A single woman can end up feeling like there's something wrong with her as she searches for a Christian man to love. It's not easy.

But God wants us to be patient. Believers have to believe that God does have a plan, that He knows what He is doing, and even though it can sometimes feel like He is taking forever, we need to trust that the happy ending will be worth it (Romans 8:28-30).

While a woman is waiting, however, it is important to keep her eyes open. She needs to be looking for five things in a potential romantic partner:

- Spiritual Compatibility
- Character Compatibility
- Emotional Compatibility

- Communication Compatibility
- Physical Attraction

First, women must look for men who are spiritually compatible. The Bible tells us in 2 Corinthians 6:14 that it is unwise to become "bound" to an unbeliever. This may seem like a good idea at the time, especially if someone is in love with an unbeliever, but it can bring incredible heartache down the road. Someone once told me that the true definition of love is wanting to help someone else grow spiritually. If a believer marries an unbeliever, that unbeliever might become resentful of the believer's love for God. An unbelieving husband can become jealous of how much time and energy a believing woman invests in God. Also, if you want to have children, you want a partner who will team with you to raise them in a Christian home, with Christian values.

Second, character compatibility. What do you think is important in life? What are your ethics? A woman of character needs to marry a man of character. If an honest woman marries a man who thinks it's okay to cheat on their taxes, this will become a major issue in their relationship. As you are getting to know a man, be sure you get to know his character. How does he behave when no one is watching him?

Emotional compatibility. Before you commit to a man, make sure that he can satisfy your emotional needs. If you need a lot of encouragement, attention, and affection, be sure that he can give it to you. If you marry a man who is not on the same emotional playing field as you are, you are just setting him, and your marriage, up for failure. Likewise, if you are not an overtly emotional person, you probably do not want to marry someone who makes decisions based on his feelings.

You've heard it before, but communication is so important in a relationship, and unfortunately, many women do not try to communicate about difficult subjects until after they are already married. You need to have those deep and challenging conversations *before* you say your vows, to make sure that you are both communicating in a way that will work for you. Different people communicate in different ways, and if a couple's two ways don't match up, they will struggle to understand each other all their lives. You need to be willing to communicate, and you need to find a man who is willing to communicate.

And finally: physical attraction. Because we are human, we often put this one at the top of the list, but it should come in last. That doesn't mean that it isn't important – it *is* important to be physically attracted to your spouse. It just means that this should not be your number one priority, and you definitely should not ignore other more important incompatibilities because you are focusing on the physical realm. If you begin in a meaningful relationship, the physical attraction will grow out of that. If you begin in physical attraction, the chemistry can fizzle out and leave you without the other connections you need.

Be patient. Pray about everything in your life, including your "love life." Believe that God has a wonderful man all picked out for you. Spend your energy loving God and God will make it happen for you. I once saw a bumper sticker that said, "A woman's heart should be so lost in God that a man needs to seek Him in order to find her." Amen.

Finding Your Path to Prosperity through God

True prosperity is about spiritual wealth. We all long for it, hope for it and most of us strive to achieve it. Perhaps we invest our money, work long hours or hope that we will win the lottery. There are so many ways we try to find what we think of as prosperity in this world, but many of us don't understand the true meaning of the word "prosperity."

God wants us to prosper in this life, but He doesn't focus solely on the monetary aspect of prosperity. To prosper actually means to have success in life, to live in the fullness of a happy, richly rewarding life. To God, prosperity isn't about how much you own or the amount of money in the bank. It is about flourishing and thriving spiritually and emotionally as well as having the comforts of life. God wants us to prosper in *all* things, not just in money.

This doesn't mean that God hates money or hates for us to live comfortably. On the contrary, He will richly reward those of us who serve Him with a loving and honest heart. God hates the *love* of money as an end in itself. If we put our desire for money above our desire to please God, we have made money an idol that we worship. No one and nothing deserves our worship except the Lord. So if you are focusing on the money as an end in itself, you will find that it quickly slips through your fingers.

To prosper in your soul, you must learn to walk with God. Praising Him and turning to Him for the answers you are seeking will nourish your soul and bring you peace – two very important aspects of Prosperity! If you are "rich in spirit," you will experience peace, happiness and contentment as you walk in the path God intended for you. He will reward you in many ways for your faithfulness and service.

> *"He continued to seek God in the days of Zacharia, who had understanding through the vision of God; and as long as he sought the Lord, God prospered him."*
>
> *–2 Chronicles 26:5*

Why Worldly Prosperity Isn't the Answer

When you focus solely on worldly prosperity, you have to sacrifice in other areas of your life. Long hours at work or too much time focusing on the pursuit of money or other worldly goods will consume you and other areas of your life will suffer a loss. You will have less time for family and friends and less time to commune with God. Your health and peace of mind will also suffer because of the stress. You may find worldly wealth, but you won't truly prosper because your life will be empty of the truly important aspects of Prosperity – God, family, friends, good health and a contented, happy heart and soul.

God doesn't want that life for you! He speaks of Prosperity as a gift that encompasses many things. If you are lonely, God will grant you companionship. Perhaps He will send the friend you have been longing to find. If you are ill, God will provide educated doctors and compassionate nurses to tend to your sickness. When you are suffering from fear, He can grant you courage. Do you see how many ways you can prosper?

> *"Do not worry then, saying, 'What will we eat?' or*
>   *'What will we drink?' or 'What will we wear for*
>   *clothing?'*
> *"For the Gentiles eagerly seek all these things; for*
>   *your heavenly Father knows that you need all these*
>   *things.*
> *But seek first His kingdom and His righteousness,*
>   *and all these things will be added to you."*
> *–Matthew 6:31-33*

The key to being truly prosperous is to understand God's reasons for what He grants you. You may ask for wealth, but it is the Lord's to grant or deny, and He knows your true heart. If you are asking for worldly prosperity for your own use, you will not be granted much. If you pray earnestly for wealth because you intend to use it to the glory of God and to help others, you will be granted a great deal. Understanding *how to use* your wealth and *how to value it* are central to what the Lord grants you.

> "....*Much will be required from everyone to whom much has been given. But even more will be demanded from the one to whom much has been entrusted.*"
>
> *-Luke 12:48*

The money and wealth of this world are to be used for God's good. They aren't goals for ourselves, but for what we can do with them. Prosperity should be a means to an end, not the end itself!

Four Steps to God's Prosperity

1. **Pray for God to grant you HIS prosperity.** Remember to ask God to grant you the kind of prosperity that is right for you. If you need peace of mind, ask that it be granted. If you are sad, ask God to guide you in the right path toward happiness. Don't assume you know what you need – turn over that decision to God, and He will grant you what you truly need.

2. **Use your prosperity wisely.** There is a lot of responsibility that comes with prosperity. Don't trust in the power of money, but use your money and your blessings toward the glory of God. You will soon find that whatever you give to others or to God comes back to you tenfold. If you hoard your prosperity, whether it is a kind word, your time or your money, you will soon find it slipping away. But when you share with an open heart and mind, you will find that the more you give, the more God will reward you.

3. **Follow God's path in all things.** God loves us and wants us to be happy, but He doesn't give without thought. He demands much of us, and we must be willing to follow His path. If we do this, we will prosper as members of His kingdom.

"My God shall supply all your need according to His riches in glory by Christ Jesus."
—Philippians 4:19

4. **Put your faith in God, not in wealth.** Remember that Prosperity is about what we truly need to be happy, and not in money as an ultimate goal. We lose so much that can enrich our lives when we turn away from God and focus on wealth. Money or possessions can be gone in an instant, but the love of the Lord is eternal. Remember this, and you will prosper as a child of God!

> *"Command those who are rich in this present world not to be arrogant nor to put their hope in wealth, which is so uncertain, but to put their hope in God, who richly provides us with everything for our enjoyment."*
>
> *−1 Timothy 6:17*

When you pray tonight, ask God to grant you the prosperity He holds in His hands. Promise the Lord that you will accept that prosperity as a great gift and use it toward His praise and the good of His people. You will soon experience the joy of prospering in all things!

The Proverbs 31 Woman

Women want to be happy, and at times this isn't easy. This is a difficult world we live in, and there's a lot to be unhappy about. But that doesn't change the fact that women still want to lead happy and fulfilling lives.

The last chapter of Proverbs can help with this. This chapter of Scripture describes the ideal woman, a "virtuous woman," a Godly woman, and guess what? She was a happy woman!

For centuries, women from all walks have looked to this woman of Proverbs for inspiration and guidance! *Why and how is this woman so happy, so fulfilled?*

Let's look at verse 13:

> "She looks for wool and flax and works with her hands in delight."

She *delights* in her work. Part of happiness, contentment, and peace lies in the simplicity of delighting in your work. No matter what that work is, one can do it as though she is doing it for God, and she can delight in it. How can a task feel like drudgery if we treat it as a delight?

In verse 17, we are told that this virtuous woman

> "girds herself with strength and makes her arms strong."

Notice that the verse does not describe a soft and needy damsel in distress! According to Holy Scripture, the ideal woman had muscles! She worked! You will be at your best when you are strong, when you work hard, when you use your strength to do good. It feels good to be healthy and strong!

Verse 20 tells us,

> "She extends her hand to the poor, and she stretches out her hands to the needy."

Many of us have learned this lesson: when you feel down, do something for someone else and you won't feel down anymore.

It couldn't be more true! Reach out to people. Extend a helping hand to those in need and the rewards will come back to you multiplied! When you help others, you honor God, and you literally help yourself. Reaching out to others is a necessary ingredient in the recipe for happiness and fulfillment!

Verse 25 tells us that,

> "Strength and dignity are her clothing, and she smiles at her future."

There's that word strength again – women of God are called to be *strong*. And this woman is *smiling* at her future. She is not tied up in worry. She is smiling. Women of God have reason to smile about their future! You have nothing to fear if you know God. You can let go of the stress that prevents you from being happy, from being at peace. You can let go by giving your worries to God.

Verses 26 and 27 read,

> "She opens her mouth in wisdom, and the teaching of kindness is on her tongue."

We can exercise a lot of control over our own lives, over our own happiness, if we exercise control over our tongues. James Chapter 3 compares our tongues to the rudders of large ships. A giant ship can be maneuvered using a small rudder. It is the same with our words. We can create better lives for ourselves simply by speaking wisdom and teaching kindness!

And in verse 30, we are told:

> "Charm is deceitful and beauty is vain, *but* a woman who fears the Lord, she shall be praised."

How much time and energy women put into being beautiful on the outside! And how unhappy some women are because they don't look the way our culture wants them to look! According to this Scripture, this is all moot – all that matters is that she fears the Lord! (And remember that "fear" in this context does not mean to crouch cowering in the corner, but to live in a state of reverent awe.) A woman who knows that God is God and believes in *His* beauty and power – *that* woman is beautiful!

And *that* woman knows peace. And *that* woman is fulfilled. And *that* woman is happy. And *that* woman can be you.

Blessed Wherever You Go

Here's what we need to remember: God *wants* to bless you.

Here's what's so hard for us to accept sometimes: God *loves* you.

Here's what we need to know about our lives: There is a *plan*!

Even before the world was made, even before you were conceived, even before you first learned about God, He knew you and He loved you and you were part of His plan. Scripture tells us that those of us who believe in Him are predestined to know Him. Before there was such a thing as time, God knew you and loved you and called you to be His child.

If we can wrap our human minds around such a majestic truth, anything that gets in our way seems petty, doesn't it?

With God's love on our side, who can be against us? The truth is that you are truly blessed wherever you go, and if you choose to trust in this blessing, to believe in this destiny, you will be opening yourself up to receiving so many more blessings! All we have to do is open our hearts and turn our minds to God and He will bless us beyond our wildest expectations.

Of course life is difficult sometimes, but that doesn't mean that God doesn't love you, or isn't blessing you at that moment. Matthew 5 tells us "Blessed are those who mourn, for they will be comforted." Many times it is the struggles that lead us to the blessings. It is the broken heart that leads us to meet the true love of our life!

Even when we are feeling down, even when we are doubting, we must still remain open to His blessings, because God will never forsake us! Scripture tells us that God uses circumstances for our own *good*!

Even when we don't understand the plan, we can still take comfort in it and believe in it, and even rejoice in it! Realize that we are *not supposed to understand* everything. Not yet. Realize that just because something doesn't *feel* like a blessing, it could be, and it most certainly will lead us to more blessings down the road.

Don't lose sight. Don't lose faith. Because God will never lose you. Even if you have tried to lose Him in the past, even if you've sometimes had doubts, even if you've done something that you think comes between you and God – He has not left you. He still loves you. He still wants to bless you.

> *"You will be blessed wherever you go, both in coming and in going"*
>
> *—Deuteronomy 28:6*

No matter what wilderness you might be wandering through. No matter what challenges you face. No matter who is against you, God is still on your side, and He wants to bless you every single day of your life. Then He wants to bless you for eternity. All you have to do is believe, and let Him do His thing. *God will bless you wherever you go.*

One Final Thought

You are very valuable to God. God loves you so much. He accepts and loves you unconditionally. Embrace the Power of Prayer daily. Set aside time alone with God in prayer daily and expect Him to speak to you. Ask God to speak to you every day and listen to Him carefully. He will teach you, strengthen you, refine you, change you and direct you. Ask God for wisdom every day so you can see things from His point of view. Read God's word daily and stand on His promises. He is faithful.

Love yourself and be happy living now and pursue your dreams and goals with passion and purpose. God's Plan for your life is always working. Trust God every day, week, month, year and season of *your* life. Call on Him to help you face every situation. Your Heavenly Father knows what's best for you.

Walk in faith, love, joy, peace and victory. With God all things are *possible. Be Blessed Wherever You Go.* May you be forever sustained by the love of God. Be encouraged - the best is yet to be in *your* life.

God sees the best in **YOU**!

"God is able to provide you with every blessing in abundance"

–2 Corinthians 9:8

About the Author

Robert Moment is an inspirational life coach, happiness expert, personal growth strategist, speaker and author of several books including **The Path to Emotional Healing- Be Happy Living Now**. Robert specializes in maximizing human potential for purpose, happiness and success.

Robert is passionate about empowering individuals on how to experience God's love, peace, power, joy and prosperity (true spiritual wealth) in their lives. Operate in the fullness of God's Plan for Your Life.

Experience Life-Changing Power...

Visit his websites:

> www.ChristianInspirational.org
> www.HowToBeHappyAgain.com

Contact Robert for Speaking, Seminar and Life Coaching Opportunities:

"Maximizing Human Potential for Purpose, Happiness and Success"

> **Email:** Robert@ChristianInspirational.org
> **Email:** Robert@HowToBeHappyAgain.com

More Information

This book is available for bulk sale. To inquire about pricing for fifty or more copies (sold at a substantial discount, non-returnable), please send an email message to:

Robert@ChristianInspirational.org

www.ingramcontent.com/pod-product-compliance
Lightning Source LLC
Chambersburg PA
CBHW061637040426

42446CB00010B/1465